Brenda
CROUCH

FIGHT FORWARD

RECLAIM THE REAL YOU

BroadStreet
PUBLISHING

BroadStreet Publishing® Group, LLC
Savage, Minnesota, USA
BroadStreetPublishing.com

FIGHT FORWARD: RECLAIM THE REAL YOU

978-1-4245-5790-5 (softcover)
978-1-4245-5791-2 (e-book)

Stock or custom editions of BroadStreet Publishing titles may be purchased in bulk for educational, business, ministry, fundraising, or sales promotional use. For information, please email info@broadstreetpublishing.com.

Cover and interior by GarborgDesign.com

Printed in the United States of America
19 20 21 22 23 5 4 3 2 1

DEDICATION

In loving memory, this book is dedicated to my mother, Verla Kathryn Sylvia, who went to be with Jesus at the inception of my first outline for this manuscript. The seeds she planted in me from early childhood and throughout my life became the fruit of love and grace, which I've poured out on every page. Her unwavering voice and her tenacious love for Jesus and the people who need Him are her legacy that will remain forever. She was my Mordecai, my intercessor, my best friend, and my biggest encourager. I miss you so very much, Mama! Until we meet again … I'll be about our Father's business.

You know you have loved someone
when you glimpse in them that
which is too beautiful to die.

GABRIEL MARCEL

CONTENTS

Foreword

The journey to becoming fully human in Christ is a lifelong one. The process is ongoing and continues until we receive our glorified bodies in the consummation of the kingdom. Until then, we are not fully there, not fully human, and not fully persons. That doesn't mean we aren't human beings; it just means we aren't *fully* human beings, and we aren't *fully* persons because we are still "on our way."

Our personhood is rooted in our creation in the image and likeness of God. Adam was created to exist for God and for others, and when Adam fell, he fell headlong into self-centered individualism. Individualism enables us to shift blame and refuse to take responsibility for the choices we make. It allows us to avoid reckoning with the resulting outcomes.

With Adam's fall, our choices became self-made, and sin left its imprint on the human race. We took a deep dive into the rebellion of individualism and independence, and we lost the essence of true humanness and personhood. The immediate results of Adam's individualism and independence were violence and death. The first family became quite dysfunctional, and the first murder was indeed fratricide: a deadly confrontation between two brothers.

Abuse is nothing new to humanity, and dysfunctional family systems are as old as time itself. The dysfunction of our individualistic, self-centered culture rears its ugly head in so many ways and causes us to lash out against others. Our words, for example, have both the ability to kill and the ability to create life. To tell a child that they will never amount to anything has a lifelong impact. It leaves a mark—an imprint that requires the salvific presence of God Himself to mend and heal (a process that can take many years). And in a society where we cater to instant gratification, the notion of healing and wholeness as a lifelong journey feeds the frenzy of our already restless and fast-paced lifestyles.

As much as we may affirm that we are new creations in Christ, we also affirm we are beset by weaknesses, and the feelings of our infirmities can often get the best of us. An infirmity is that which takes away our strength. All sorts of things throughout our journey rob us of our strength and challenge our ability to move forward. None of us arrive at adulthood without wounds, even if we were raised in a Christian home. Brokenness and beauty coexist in all of us, and the reason is simple: sin is still present; good and evil still coexist, and we are fallible and flawed and in need of grace to be and to become who the Father intended in Christ by His Spirit.

Our journeys leave some of us more wounded than others and vulnerable to the experience of victimization. Depending on the degree of victimization, the innocent party may suffer great trauma, and with great trauma often comes a profound level of shock and numbness. Many victims subconsciously freeze their pain, and the process of thawing out their emotions and allowing themselves to feel again can take years. Denial and anger are often present simply because it can be far too painful for the victim to admit the wound ever happened in the first place.

But there is hope. In Jesus we see true personhood, true humanity, and the opposite of egocentric individualism. Jesus isn't out to "get"; He exists to give. Christ was the victim of the worst and most cruel hate crime in all of history, and through His own death, burial, resurrection, and ascension, He established a pathway for victims to become victors in and through Him.

I have known Brenda Crouch for a number of years, and I have been deeply impacted by her life story. I am moved by the way the Lord has navigated her through pain to become an agent of the Spirit's healing grace to others who have suffered wounding. In her brand-new book *Fight Forward: Reclaim the Real You*, Brenda makes her life an open book. Her transparency is an open window that lets the fresh air of heaven into the dark rooms of our isolation and pain, where our wounds have grown foul and festered. Her story will not only draw you in, but it will also invite you to explore the pain you have endured and help lead you to Jesus, His healing presence, and His grace.

If you are reading this book, it is precisely because you are ready to get your "fight" back—the good fight of faith, which refuses to settle for less than the journey to a future immersed in Jesus' glorious inheritance. It is time to move forward and reclaim the real you, and this book is as good a place to start as I know to help you take your first step.

Dr. Mark J. Chironna
Church On The Living Edge
Mark Chironna Ministries

Fight Forward:
Reclaim the Real You

For the last twenty years, I have been steered internally by essentially one question: Do you truly understand the salvation of your soul and how it affects your real life? With every tragic loss this question has resonated more deeply, and my journey to the answers has been long, often difficult, and repetitious. But the aspects of my life that I once had no power to change have been drastically corrected, and I have been categorically transformed in the light of truth. The work of the Spirit of God becomes evident when we notice a difference in how we respond to what once seduced us, controlled us, and even crushed us.

As I prepared to write this book, I lost my mother quite tragically and unexpectedly. It was a significant, life-altering event that rocked me to the core of my being, and the months that followed were filled with many tearful hours asking God for the courage and strength to tell my story. The love I have for both of my parents, my entire family, and our lifelong friends makes the delicate nature of information pertaining to my past difficult to unveil. However, I do so for the sake of setting others free from lies. Wisdom requires prudence, and this is not a book of therapy. I'm past that. Out of obedience to the call of God, I relinquish my dangerous transparency for one purpose only: to offer a place of safety and compassion for the reader who might be struggling with similar issues. I do not believe you have picked this book up by accident, and it is my prayer that you will feel the presence of the Holy Spirit, who is a comforter, revealer, and constant companion for the journey I will ask you to bravely take with me.

It has never been my intent to hurt anyone from my past, nor is it now. I also want to honor both my parents who stand with the great cloud of witnesses in heaven praying me through this and cheering me on for my stance against the kingdom of darkness and its deceptive clutches over the minds and identities of desperate hurting people. I honor both my mother and father for what they did right with the limited knowledge they possessed, and I pray for those from my past who still have time to find their way to freedom. I have purposely kept names private and chosen to omit much of the salacious information that deeply affected my journey for the sake of living persons.

Like my father, some of us have come from iniquitous bloodlines that have held us in chains without our knowledge. As I wrote the last chapter of this book, by God's exquisite timing, I was connected to a second cousin from my paternal ancestry when she reached out to me after a DNA test matched us. She is a feisty eighty-six-year-old today with a brilliant mind, and she is a follower of Christ! Her personal accounts of our family history opened a floodgate of information, which only confirmed my understanding of family curses and the iniquities that went back generations beyond the ones I already knew about. A history of domestic violence, murder, and cover-up, repeated generational incest, alcoholism, gambling, and musical talent had left their traces in my blood. Ironically, people of great faith who loved my father and invested their whole hearts toward blessing him make up the other side of my ancestry. They were preachers, pastors, missionaries, and entrepreneurial hard workers. The prayers of these saints have brought the women of my family before the courtrooms of heaven, where the blood of Jesus has redeemed the wrongs and continues to break chains in and through us.

My honest motivation for telling my story after years of repeated violations by various individuals, including sexual assault in school and in the workplace, is not to simply say, "Me too." I'm here to say, "But God!" We need answers to annihilate the epidemic of dishonor and abuse, and we need them quickly. Healing and restoration are not only available for victims, because God loves both victims and victimizers. He offers freedom to everyone imprisoned by dark secrets. The real enemy is the one who controls your soul through a lie, and in this book I intend to unmask him. It's imperative to understand the roots of such abuse and how that, historically, religion has often failed to rightly portray the love and mercy of Christ to those who need it most. However, the outrage of culture has brought a season of reformation upon us.

If you are not a believer in Christ, I pray you will see from my story that we are all flawed as humans who are continually being transformed into the image of who Jesus truly is. Becoming a child of God happens in an instant, but becoming who we were meant to be takes a lifetime. Those who let God heal them will, in turn, heal others. If you are a church leader, my experiences with intimidation, manipulation, hiding behind false projections, and bad advice will equip you with insights to better understand the need for arming your ministry with solid life-changing programs focused on healing and restoring people to their divine purpose. These wounded souls who may not always feel welcomed into your circles are, in reality, future ministers. They have the potential to grow and expand the vision God has given you, and your purpose in His kingdom, if you'll recognize and value them for who they are meant to be in Christ.

If you are a millennial standing on the edge of your dreams, may the price I paid to find my identity be a testimony of God's faithfulness to you and a weapon of truth against the deception of culture as you pursue your real destiny in Christ alone. If you are a victim of abuse, I pray you will find the faith to believe in greater things for your life and the strength to follow Jesus, even when His path appears daunting. You have a purpose, and God has a plan for your life. Trust Him and He will not fail you! Just as my pursuit of the meaning of salvation has led me to authentic personhood in Christ, I pray that you will also discover your true salvation as His life works itself into every detail of your being. You were worth every sacrifice to Jesus, and because of His abiding love in me, you are worth every sacrifice that I have ever given for the honor of pointing the way to a fully restored identity.

"The LORD bless you and keep you; the LORD make his face shine upon you, and be gracious to you; the LORD turn his face toward you and give you peace" (Numbers 6:24–26).

1

||||||||||||||||||||||||||||

Seventeen Days

My sister and I had just landed at Oakland International Airport, eager to make the commute over the Altamont Pass to the Central Valley of California where our dad awaited our arrival. Those trips from Dallas to California were much more frequent after my father had been diagnosed with idiopathic pulmonary fibrosis (for which there is no known cause or cure). It had been an excruciating six-month battle since the previous summer when our long-time family doctor announced to us that Dad had seen his last Christmas, but holding onto our faith in God, we refused to accept his early death sentence or the given time line.

As determined ambassadors of hope, we committed ourselves to finding alternative treatments while we prayed for a miracle. We believed that God could heal him, but despite all the faith we could muster and the arsenal of holistic medicines that we convinced him to try, we faced the dreaded process of having to say goodbye. By immersing ourselves in family history and childhood memories, we did our best to maintain our sanity by coasting through much of the process on emotional autopilot.

At the end of a two-hour drive with a family friend who had faithfully arranged our transportation and provided cheerful conversation, the moment of truth finally arrived. Nervously, we entered the building. A distinctive sterile smell lingered in the hushed atmosphere that demanded reverence from all who arrived. The Hospice House had a warm, residential feel that was strangely juxtaposed by intermittent hospital technology. It was a weird combination that seemed to probe at the indistinguishable sorrow lingering just beneath the surface of our smiles. For now, this place would be our indefinite home away from home, and the only way we knew to avoid getting swallowed up by our fear of the unknown was to keep a positive disposition.

I had never set foot in a Hospice House before that day. I'd only heard about the significant role they play in assisting terminally ill patients and their grieving families with the painful process of passing from earth to eternity. It's a little daunting, in hindsight, to recognize the extent of my lingering youthful ignorance that still occupied my attention well into adulthood. There were major blind spots limiting my range of sight when it came to navigating life's sudden turns. I now realize that it was my deep and familiar sense of denial that carried me into the uncharted terrain of parental bereavement, but I was definitely in line for a major awakening. God was about to clear some considerable obstructions from my path that had impeded my perspective. Gracefully He made the process of my awakening a merciful one that came layer by layer.

I could almost feel His tangible arms enveloping me during my father's transition, like a tender lullaby of sweet mercy in my darkest hours. Carefully He began the pruning process, slowly snipping away the brambles that had entangled my soul for far too long. Night after night my sister and I lay on hard cots with thin cotton blankets that didn't keep us very warm. Being a medical facility, the temperature was always kept quite cool, but after a while, certain members of the night staff took a liking to us and began offering multiple blankets fresh out of the warmer to make our stay there a little more comfortable. It was unusual for family members to remain so close 24/7, and though it wasn't against the rules, they were not set up for long-term overnighters. But we weren't going anywhere. We were in it for the duration.

Like my sister, I was less concerned about my personal discomfort and more brokenhearted watching my father's slow decline. He seemed more like a compliant little boy than the father we knew. Often at night he would call out in the darkness, "Hello … is anybody there?" I felt the fear in his voice and wanted to cry, but instead I tried to be strong as my sister and I tag-teamed, each of us barely sleeping. Whenever he would cry out at night, one of us would rush to his side to comfort him and tend to his needs. Based on the distress he exhibited, I got an eerie feeling that when he awoke from his medicated sleep in pitch darkness, he was questioning whether he had crossed over into eternity. He didn't have the deep peace I'd hoped to witness after a life of serving God. That made me hurt so badly for him—so much so that I'd lie on my cot and cry silently in the dark once he had been consoled.

As insomnia stole coveted sleep from my eyes, I remembered the man I had idolized but also deeply longed to understand better. He was the life of the party in every setting, sporting quick jokes and movie star good looks (which were still very much intact). But the familiar persona that everyone loved had suddenly become a thin veil for the pain that I knew he was dealing with. Dad had a genius talent for music and could play almost every instrument he tried simply by ear. His vocal tone was like liquid gold. His music made a lot of people happy for as long as he lived, and I was always so proud. Music was an intrinsic part of our family bond, and watching my dad perform was nothing short of magical. He was such a powerful force in our lives that I didn't notice the poverty of his soul hiding behind the charisma until I saw the same lack within my own somewhere in my middle-adult years.

As a child, my relational dynamics with people became difficult as I withdrew in confusion, trying my best to survive the classism and social dynamics of school. Then in high school, I was determined to make a mark for myself. There are gaps of time from my childhood that I cannot remember. During the time of my father's passing, I felt like an incomplete puzzle that was missing too many pieces to form a picture of substance. Some memories, however, remained intact as a significant part of my past. One cherished memory centered on a rare day when my dad joined my sister and me for a bike ride. Usually our time with him was spent watching him play his guitar or watching TV together, so this day was a special treat.

He decided to ride my bike since it was the bigger of the two and encouraged me to hop on the handlebars. They were the long scooped kind from the 1970s and seemed like the perfect way to share a ride. But I wasn't very comfortable, so I ran inside the house to grab a pillow off the sofa to cushion my seat. *Voila!* We were ready to ride. My younger sister rode her bike next to us, and she and Dad started racing with one another. I got nervous and asked Dad to slow down. When he hit the brakes, I went soaring into the air and landed about five feet in front of him on the asphalt.

I tumbled a few times and quickly regained my stance, realizing I had road rash from top to bottom. My chin, my elbows, my knees, my shins, and my hands were all skinned deep enough to leave scars, but my biggest concern was that it might cause my dad to never ride with us again, so I ignored my pain and very quickly yelled out, "I still love you, Daddy! I still love you!" He felt just awful about it and scooped me up with a big hug. Then he took me into the house where Mom cleaned and nursed my wounds. It was all so fun until the sudden hard landing that ended it all. Oh how we laughed and screamed wildly that beautiful summer day, but I don't remember ever riding bicycles with Dad again after that.

Another distinct memory from that same year involved my childish attempt to stow away in the back of my father's work truck for the long commute to his construction job at an Indian reservation. Dad was a tile layer, and he would be gone for a week or more at a time due to how far away his jobsite was. I later learned this was the time frame in which he'd become addicted to gambling. He never drank alcohol because he hated what he saw it do to his parents and its effect on their family, but the dynamics of addiction were still a part of his life and the lure of fast money must have gripped him. I had written a note to my mother that morning so she would not worry about me as I packed a little blue suitcase with my pajamas and a hairbrush, among a few other items that I considered necessities for a week's journey. I figured once Dad realized I was with him, it would be too late to turn around and I'd be his buddy for the remainder of his time there. It was the perfect plan!

My plan was hugely interrupted, however, when my mother found the note I'd left her before we even pulled out of the driveway. At times I think I was a pretty cute kid, but there are other times I just roll my eyes and laugh. My dad was the hero I longed for, and I wanted more time with him. Now I realize he most likely didn't know how to connect on an emotional level due to his own childhood. I do know that he tried though, because he told us that he loved us and was proud of us often—especially when my sister and I got older and became pageant queens who could sing like birds. Dad always made the audience laugh with a funny line about feeding us Hartz canary bird seed when we were little to condition our voices.

My mother was a spiritual and emotional nurturer, bringing a positive influence into my dad's life with her kindness and confidence in his abilities. She provided a depth of love that he'd never had as a kid at home, but he was often emotionally unavailable, even for her. Dad's distance didn't seem abnormal to me in my growing-up years. I actually thought it was just how men were, and I was fascinated with understanding the mind of a man as a result. It did make vulnerability with him very difficult, however—especially when broaching subjects like boys, a broken heart, or female issues, etc. We pretty much avoided those types of things with Dad. As a matter of fact, my sister and I just knew he would disapprove if we talked about boys, so we kept our taboo thoughts hidden. I remember keeping my eyes straight ahead when a cute boy walked by in a restaurant because my dad was present and I didn't want to get his look of disapproval. Mom, on the other hand, wanted us to open up to her so that she could guide us with her wisdom. We did talk to Mom usually, but some subjects were just too embarrassing to explore despite her determined effort to offer us advice.

Well into my late twenties, I was troubled by a variety of reoccurring dreams that were very traumatic. My father was always present in these dreams and always appeared to be overcome with shame. I reasoned that was because he must have known or seen something that happened to me and failed to protect me from it. The dreams were like fragmented scenes from a movie, and I would always awaken with a sickening feeling of revulsion in the deepest part of my being. I loved my dad, but I was not comfortable sharing these dreams with anyone. For years I compartmentalized them in a private box of shame. I didn't understand them until a critical point in my life when I sought the help of a licensed counselor to cope with depression and anxiety. In the process of therapeutic counseling, he probed about some of my issues with domestic abuse and my emotional survival mechanisms.

When he asked me whether I had been sexually molested, I stammered nervously over the question and my heart beat rapidly. A very uneasy feeling of shame swept over my mind. I hesitantly described some incidents from my later childhood that had taken place in the home of a church member. My mother, thankfully, put a stop to it and protected us from the worst of it. I realized I should inform him of my reoccurring dreams because, although I wasn't sure what they meant, I felt they were a loud signal that something else was wrong. He told me that I was a textbook example of someone who had been sexually molested as a child. He also explained that some young children emotionally split from the trauma, burying the memory so deep in their subconscious that they cognitively erase it or shut it down for survival. The fact that I had developed this very sophisticated defense mechanism was a dead giveaway that I'd been abused.

I didn't like the unraveling feeling of someone seeing through me when I had convinced myself that I was wise and authentic. Perhaps at the core of my being the elements of wisdom and authenticity were present, but it was also cluttered with façades and counterfeit projections that I used to counteract my self-hatred. I'm convinced that it was strictly by grace and my mama's prayers that God helped me to not only survive the devastation of my shame but also walk through the process of healing with the assistance of the Holy Spirit and good strong counsel.

For years I wondered about the nagging question that haunted me in my nightmares. It pricked at my soul more heavily as I got older, and in a brave moment, I asked God to show me the truth about what was missing from the memories of my early childhood in His perfect timing. At one point I tried to bring up the subject with my father because we seemed much closer in my adult years than we'd ever been. By this time though, he and Mom were no longer together. Years of strain and his infidelity had taken its toll on their marriage. During that season of our lives we had a fun tradition of meeting on Saturday mornings for breakfast and black coffee. I always loved coffee because he loved it, and to this day, having breakfast on a Saturday morning tucked away in the corner of some diner feels like coming home.

It was my desperate hope that perhaps together we could both come free from the burden of whatever secrets lay behind us and build a better relationship going forward. Awkwardly, I spit the difficult and heavy words out of my mouth, trying to put us both at ease while describing the repetitious dreams that I'd been having. They always involved him having a look of shame and disgust as he shook his low-hanging head and tried to tell me something. "Dad, I know that I was sexually molested by an adult as a little girl, and I know exactly what happened. I'm just not certain who did it. I've buried the memory, and I'm hoping that you might help me figure this out."

What had been hidden all those years was now trying to come into the light, and I was finally giving it permission so I could be released from what had hindered me for so long. "Do you think it could have possibly been a family member?" I asked. Both my uncles on his side of the family had been inappropriate at moments toward my sister and me in our teen years and early twenties. Dad was often present when they made sexual innuendos and coarse jokes around us, but he always seemed to blow that stuff off as just their crazy antics and acted like he was ashamed of their behaviors. I'd also heard about some of the generational incest that had taken place within his family, so I was simply putting two and two together. I never understood why he hadn't been more protective or quick to come to our defense over these subtle violations that left my sister and me feeling quite powerless and awkward, but I never knew how to talk about it either.

I don't remember the specific words Dad used in response to my inquiry that morning over breakfast, only that he shrugged off my questions and the details of each dream, rapidly changing the subject to something benign. I followed the flow of conversation as he guided it elsewhere and decided that it must have just been too uncomfortable for him to talk about. My nagging questions weren't going anywhere however, and I later gave pause to why he would not have cared more to discuss potential perpetrators who might have violated his little girl. I was so accustomed to brushing things off and betraying myself in every relationship that I had trouble with real confrontation or asking for accountability from others. These traits made me a target for easy manipulation.

Not only was I terrified of the possible answers to what privately plagued me, but I also couldn't bear the thought of losing what little relationship I had worked so hard to earn with my daddy. Sometimes the truth coming out leaves you feeling like you want to put the toothpaste back in the tube—a virtually impossible task once it has been released. Years went by before the subject ever resurfaced again, but I found my peace by placing the issue in the hands of my heavenly Father, knowing that I could trust His perfect timing and faithful companionship in the process of finding truth and restoring my soul.

Healing is not an instant work, whether physical, emotional, or spiritual. It is a progressive process that consists of significant moments of deep revelation and putting new truth into practice. These are the building blocks of freedom, and the pace of progress is sometimes dependent on the readiness of other individuals or loved ones who play a significant role in the course of your healing. Part of my personal healing process involved facing the reality that my father was a fragile human and not the superstar I had made him out to be. Just a month prior to dad's admittance into hospice care, this harsh reality abruptly confronted me. The man I'd worshiped and considered to be invincible since childhood had no more fight left in him. It was time for me to quit preaching to him about *choosing life* and finally accept *his* will in the matter.

The news wasn't easy for either of us as he called me to his bedside that mid-December morning to tell me he was too weak to fight any longer and was giving up on living. I wept bitterly with my head on his chest as nothing but the sound of our sobbing and his uncontrolled coughing filled the room. Once we both were able to compose ourselves, he quietly said, "Daddy doesn't have much to give you girls, but I have saved a small amount of cash in my safe to help cover the expense of your flights, and I want you to have my jewelry box."

I was quite familiar with his wooden jewelry box as a kid because it sat on my parents' dresser and exploring its contents made me feel closer to my dad. With a grateful heart I reached to pick it up off his night-stand. The lifetime we had shared suddenly rushed through my mind. Knowing the essence of my father was contained in that familiar little box with the etched glass lid, his keepsakes spoke to me as I slowly sifted through them one by one. As scenes of my childhood flooded my mind, I now saw these things from a different perspective. I saw them through the eyes of a grown woman who had been ransacked by years of denial and abuse, and I could not believe that the man I considered to be larger than life would very soon become a memory and my only tangible reminder of him was going to be reduced to a small lacquered jewelry box filled with fading mementos of yesteryear.

The six-month process of our long goodbye involved making new memories and exchanging fresh devotions of love. They were now the sustaining link joining our fragmented hearts and questionable past to our present hope in Christ. We sat together in a house where people go to die, waiting … just waiting, loving, and reminiscing. For over two weeks Dad's hospice room was filled with so much love and laughter that the administrative staff and nurses became emotionally attached to our family. They shared with us that they were very careful about avoiding such attachment as it made their jobs easier to do, but this was different. Dad had a wonderful array of visitors that included the hospice chaplain, the pastor from a local assembly, lifelong friends, cousins, aunts, and uncles who gathered around him for hours at a time.

My sister and I sang the old hymns that we'd grown up singing together, and we successfully maintained a happy, lighthearted disposition by staying in the moment, knowing that very soon those moments would vanish from us forever. When his medications were increased only a couple days later, Dad lost consciousness but seemed to be listening more intently than ever as we sang a familiar gospel song that our family had often sung together. Gathered around his bedside, my sister and I, along with our cousins, enjoyed a joyful and meaningful moment until he unexpectedly began to cry like a little child. His countenance changed to one of deep anguish, and his inconsolable sobbing interrupted the mood of our sentimental singing.

Looking me squarely in the eye as if no one else was there, I suddenly became frightened by the look on his face, and everyone held their breath. Barely managing to utter the words through quivering lips, his eyes still locked with mine, he cried out with a broken voice, "I am *so* sorry!" Immediately, his wife of four years sprang from her seat and rushed to his side to pat his back and calm him. "You have nothing to be sorry for, you are a good and godly man," she said. He failed to respond as his eyes and attention remained locked with mine. The room was absolutely still, and our hearts were held captive. I *knew* that this was a moment of truth for my father, who had done his best to maintain a godly life on the faulty foundation of his wounded childhood but had failed to find peace in his own human strength.

I saw in him a precious life that had never fully experienced the amazing grace God has given to us all. Finally my father was courageous enough to crack open the door to his freedom, exposing his most dreaded secret before he died. It was the answer to all the questions I had quietly prayed about in my private sanctuary, and I knew this could finally release us both from our prison of shame. I did not in any way want to hurt or humiliate my dad, who I knew had also been abused as a child, so I gently asked everyone in the room to allow me to privately have his ear as I leaned down to whisper, "Daddy, I already *know*, and I have forgiven you. Now you need to forgive yourself!" He sobbed from such a deep and broken place of remorse, brutally choking on his words as he said, "I don't think I can …" My heart broke for him as I realized the horrible shame he had carried all those years.

Suddenly the emotional distance that had always been between us seemed to vanish, and I began to understand the reasons that he hid behind his beautiful persona. I took his hand and said, "Daddy, do you believe Jesus shed His blood to forgive you and set you free?" He said, "Yes, I hope so." His words were broken and breathy as he faced his greatest fear. This was a man who sang of God's love and grace, yet he trembled in his final moments, wondering if he could be forgiven.

I asked, "Will you pray a prayer with me if I lead you?" He agreed as he continued to weep, and together we prayed, "Heavenly Father, you are a good and merciful father, and I come before you in the name of your Son, Jesus. Today, I step into the light of truth and ask your forgiveness as I lay all my shame and all my brokenness at your feet. I believe and I receive your forgiveness for the sin that I've carried, and I thank you for your sacrifice of love. Receive my spirit into your arms!" As we echoed those last words in prayer, I had a vision of Jesus. I literally saw Him in the spirit, standing at heaven's gate with arms wide open and the biggest smile on His face, the first of many brethren welcoming my daddy to his final home.

I knew that my dad finally had the peace he needed and was ready to meet Jesus because he was receiving the love he had always longed for but never really knew as a son of the Most High. It was a total of seventeen days that we spent with him in that room before he passed on, and many of us wondered at one point if it was a premature call to admit him into hospice care. Now I am thankful to know it was a gift from God to us all. I believe my dad was holding onto life this side of heaven, merely to soak up the last bits of our love and to ask forgiveness from me and from Jesus before making his final voyage home.

The day of his passing finally came, and we were all ready to let him go. Prior to slipping out of consciousness, Dad had asked my sister and me to sing an old country and western gospel song called "Gentle Stranger" at the time that he crossed over, and we kept that promise to him. It was difficult to sing under those emotional conditions, but music was such a huge part of what drew us all together so it only seemed like a natural transition to honor him that way. After a while his breathing became more belabored, and then he struggled for his final breath. But as hard as he worked for it, it did not come. His eyes slightly opened as his chest bowed upward in one final gasp, and then he was gone.

Tears flooded my face as my sister and I began to worship the Lord in unison, knowing that our daddy was finally whole and finally home. At that very moment I experienced an unexplainable phenomenon as heaven's glory touched the earth. I felt a physical shift inside my body as if my inner compass suddenly clicked on and something awakened on the inside of me. Then I heard the Spirit of the Lord say to me in a whisper, "Don't be afraid, I will be with you!" Suddenly I knew I would be okay. I had lamented for so many months, telling God, "I'm not ready to lose my daddy, please don't take him." I thought surely I would be lost without him.

It is with tears in my eyes that I remember those final moments with our dad, but the truth is, I had been lost in an emotional maze for so many years, desperately seeking the way to freedom, but God was healing and preparing me for the next part of my journey. In the years that prefaced my father's death, I had to face the truth of my own impoverished soul as my heavenly Father rewrote my future within the dark space of my tiny cocoon. Perhaps at the moment of my father's passing, I took my own new breath of life, engaging my inner compass to recognize that I was no longer existing but ready to thrive and trust that God would be faithful to finish the work He'd already begun in my life. I was at peace knowing I could rejoice because my dad had finally found his freedom, but it would take me a while longer to fully discover mine.

2

||||||||||||||||||||||||||

Dismantling the Crown

There she is ... Miss America! Every wide-eyed little girl in the 1970s was glued to the television when Bert Parks serenaded the newly crowned queen of the country. She was a vision of what we all aspired to be, the "dream of a million girls," Bert sang as we imagined what it would be like to wear her crown. Taking the Atlantic City runway, she convinced us that she was "walking on air," and I'm quite certain that a million dreams were born as the glorious tradition was broadcast into our ordinary living rooms each year.

I never owned a dime store tiara as a kid, let alone had the opportunity to see the real thing up close and personal, but everything sparkly had a magical effect on me. I distinctly remember sneaking Mom's tin foil from the kitchen drawer a few times too many to create my own make-believe version. My imagination soared with endless possibilities of who I'd like to be, and I was just as enamored by Dorothy's ruby red slippers in *The Wizard of Oz*.

Perhaps those shimmering imitations were just pale reflections, pointing me to the divine light that we all innately search for. It's only natural that we find shiny things attractive. We were made to be the house of God, and He is the ultimate source of light. But sadly, we often become sidetracked by our emphasis on external appearances instead of experiencing the true power of His Light within us.

Such was my case as my faulty foundation led me to fixate on projecting a loveable image instead of just accepting myself for who I was. This was the setup for attracting the wrong kind of people into my life—people who demanded perfection and probed at my gnawing insecurities, which drove me to destruction. I worked very hard to achieve a glamorous image, but this naive girl was forced to discover the truth that there was no Wizard behind my curtain of lies.

It was no secret to anyone who knew my family during my adolescent years that my parents had raised my sister and me to be good girls, and they encouraged us to believe we could achieve anything with the talents God gave us. They didn't want to hold us back in the ways they had been hindered by their parents—through verbal abuse in my father's case and religious legalism in my mother's.

However, the seed of a shame-based identity had already taken root as a result of the sexual abuse in my early childhood, and that lie had been growing for a while in the soil of my soul. My father's inability to truly understand his own value reinforced the same deception in him that was growing within me. While my mother struggled in a different way with her own self-image and appearance, both of their identity issues affected my own values.

Both my parents took special pride in our morals, physical beauty, and multiple talents, which I believe represented a second chance at the opportunities they longed to achieve vicariously through both my sister and me. I know they had only good intentions behind their frequent affirmations of pride in our abilities, but this became the standard by which I defined my worth, despite my love and dedication to the Lord.

My ability to perform and be a good girl was where I placed my confidence and personal value. My concept of God's grace and love was only based on what I was taught, as I was yet to receive it straight from my Father God. My mother sincerely taught us all about God's love and grace, but sometimes it takes the hard lessons of life's consequences to actually perceive the true value of His forgiveness.

As a keen observer of the shifting dynamics between my parents, I noticed certain fractures in their relationship but did not understand them from a psychological or spiritual perspective. I perceived my father as the one who had all the fun while my mother was the responsible workhorse. Naturally, I wanted a shortcut to happiness rather than a hard life, so I followed my father's example and relied on the talents, charm, and good looks that I was born with to put me on the fast-track toward my dreams.

I didn't realize my plan would backfire or that I still needed to develop the kind of discipline that leads to success and fulfillment. I was convinced that my moral character was enough to earn God's favor. But life would come to teach me that the components of good character are comprised of much more than moral fortitude or simply *telling* the truth. I had to learn the value of disciplined focus and endurance.

There are many great qualities that I credit my mother with teaching me, like honor and the gift of encouragement. She was a woman filled with such grace and compassion, but having been a victim of severe religious abuse, she was often misunderstood because of her skewed sense of boundaries. This taught me that the method of communication is vital to the effectiveness of the content. Using the wrong tools to convey the truth often sabotages our good intentions and renders us unproductive, even if our motives are pure.

On a couple of rare occasions my mother opened up about the religious control wielded over her by her parents and grandparents, who meant well but sometimes erred in their judgment. The truth was heartbreaking, but it helped me understand my mother better as I recognized her amazing heart to honor them and the degree of her forgiveness.

One story my mother told us about her childhood took place on Christmas morning when her grandmother ripped a string of shiny new pearls straight off her neck and threw them into the fire because she believed it was a sin to wear jewelry. I was aghast to think of the tension in the room and how my mother's heart must have shattered that day. A precious gift, which was meant to bring joy from her mother, was destroyed for the sake of enforcing a stronghold of shame and legalism over everyone.

Another incident that will forever be burned into my memory involved my mother eating squash at the dinner table as a little girl. She told her father that she wasn't feeling well. Though he was a very loving and tender man in many ways, he was also a strict disciplinarian, and his judgment in this particular situation wasn't the right one. He forced my mother to eat all of it despite her complaints of being ill, and she vomited everything she ate back onto her plate. Immediately, her dad made her eat what she had just vomited because he somehow interpreted her vomiting as an act of rebellion against his authority.

When my mother told me that story, we were sitting at the dinner table eating yellow squash, which must have triggered the memory for her. I was stunned by the willpower she must've had to ever enjoy the vegetable again. It became apparent to me that her strict upbringing as a pastor's kid had developed her strong will to walk the line, but in her heart she sincerely did it for the Lord.

I can't express how much I admire her willingness to let go of religious legalism and find freedom in the grace of Jesus on her journey. It was a long and slow process to overcome her former bondage, but she always pursued Him with tremendous joy. Obviously my mother's misunderstandings of acceptance, along with my father's emotional unavailability and abuse, influenced my own cognitive perception of God's love for me. I am profoundly moved when I think of how polarized my perception of my heavenly Father was and how long I tried to please Him without knowing or understanding the true nature of His love for me.

This flawed collection of beliefs caused me to attract the type of guys who only saw me as arm candy in adulthood. Instead of being valued for my integrity and inner beauty, they only appreciated me for how I made them feel. Despite the emphasis placed at home on moral purity and maintaining virginity, I completely missed the critical perspective of why my virginity was valuable outside of being a *gift* to my husband and that I'd be fulfilling God's will for me.

My lack of comprehension combined with the shame that was tied to my identity as a victim of sexual abuse caused cracks in the foundation of my self-perceived core value. I had become emotionally fractured as a child, never realizing that I vacillated between two conflicting personas for many years. This felt like a fight between the *two of me*, and it seemed to be magnified in the area of my talent for singing. Most likely this was because I'd tied my identity to music and performing.

Desperate to feel special, I thought I'd found my purpose when I was fourteen years old and discovered that I could hold an audience captive when I sang. I had been singing solos since the age of two in churches and other venues with my family, but when I was asked to sing a solo for a school concert that year, it was the first time my peers heard me sing. I was accustomed to the church crowds and gospel music, but performing a secular song for an unfamiliar audience was thrilling, and I was ready to show them that I knew what I was doing.

In those days we didn't have a lot of extra money for new clothes unless it was budgeted for back-to-school season, but Mom was creative and she made me the prettiest dress with some cool aqua floral fabric that she'd stashed away. I felt so special as I took center stage to assert my expertise with the microphone. It was a full house, and the atmosphere was electric as Mom proudly watched from the audience.

As I belted out the final lyric to a passionate song about life, love, and significance, the audience's reaction overwhelmed me. Every person from the main floor to the balcony stood up and was screaming and cheering for an unusually long period of time. Their ovation was more than I had expected, and that's all it took for the entertainment bug to bite me hard. From that moment on, I knew I had been born to sing.

Singing became so much a part of my identity that at one time I thought life without music would be worse than death itself. Besides Jesus, it was the most common bond in our family and an intrinsic part of my happiest memories. Through the years, I worked very hard at perfecting my talent as a performer and pursued theater acting. My natural ability for singing and dancing landed me lead roles in coveted musical productions. After winning a few local talent shows, I was invited to compete in the local Miss America franchise pageant.

Enthusiastically, I took the plunge and quickly adapted to this new platform where I could showcase my talent. When the time came to decide what song I would sing for competition, I was torn between a popular secular song and the gospel music that my family was so proud of. I chose to make my mother proud and hoped it might even earn points with God when I sang something from the contemporary Christian music charts by Amy Grant. I continued this gospel tradition for the remainder my pageant career.

I'll never forget the first time I was announced a winner. Crocodile tears streamed down my face as I took my coronation walk on the runway. It was magical to wear a real crown that shined like diamonds, and I thought, *Something extraordinary has happened to me, and I really am walking on air!* While there were many positive aspects to my involvement in the program, it also proved to reinforce my false beliefs, coaxing me even further into projecting a more perfect image.

I took professional modeling courses and learned all the tricks of stage makeup from Nevada's showgirls. My stage wardrobe was custom made in Las Vegas by one of Elvis' personal seamstresses, and I was grateful to have been born with the right figure for those beautiful sequined gowns. I was morphing into something glamorous, and I worked hard to achieve the ideal image. But in trying so hard to be a winner, I continued to lose sight of who I really was in the process.

I didn't want to be the girl who identified with shame and self-rejection anymore; I wanted to be a queen. I even spiritualized my goal, believing it to be God's will for my life. Placing fourth runner-up at my first Miss Nevada pageant only amplified the encouragement of those around me, and I decided to compete again after skipping a year to attend Bible college with my scholarships.

The second time around I was in it to win it, taking the preliminary talent award and nailing my interview with very high scores. I came so close to wining the state title that year, but my dream of Atlantic City was suddenly dashed when half a point's difference made me the first runner-up instead of the title holder.

I went on to carry the Miss Nevada title as a contestant in the National Sweetheart pageant, which was tradition, but my confidence had been deflated, and I spiraled into a pit of emotional confusion. The Miss America crown actually represented something that I personally needed in order to prove my value (to myself more than anyone else).

In my heart I wanted to believe in great things, but I was convinced on a deeper level that nothing good would ever truly come to me. I was the culmination of my parents' contrasting personalities, which shaped my identity. Mom believed nothing was impossible, always encouraging our potential, but Dad had a more negative perspective about his own identity. While he proudly boasted of our talents, he carried the memory of his parents telling him that he would never amount to anything.

Somehow the power of evil words had broken the barriers of generational walls, and though they had never been spoken over me, they found a way to poison me as well. Its no wonder the Bible emphasizes the Father's blessing as such an important component of our identity. Some fathers love with emotional affection but are not fully equipped to give their children the blessing of a whole and healthy identity. Sadly, the root of my father's identity was sabotaged by the devil's lies, resulting in my own twisted perspective.

We all tend to compensate for our insecurities through unreliable belief systems, which support the illusion of an identity but will never truly fix what lies beneath the fragile surface. Until we allow God's love to comprehensively redefine us, we cannot truly know who we are. I'm grateful now for the experiences I gleaned from pageant programs because they gave me the skills for job interviews, social etiquette, stage presence, and a decent grasp of current events. But I'm also thankful that, by God's design, I had to dig deeper in every area of my personal development to discover His true purpose for my life.

After relinquishing my crown to my younger sister, who took the local title that year, I ventured out on my own. But conflict arose between my father and me over a new boyfriend. At twenty-one years old, I was desperate for independence and battled for control over my life decisions. I decided to relocate to California. I enjoyed living in my native state and even toyed with the idea of competing again for Miss California, but it wasn't long before my attention was commandeered by the allure of another relationship, which gave me a new sense of purpose.

Abandoning the pageant ship all together, I jumped headlong into the idea of marriage. The previous year I had been introduced to an evangelist preacher from Texas while attending Capital Bible Institute in Sacramento, so I rationalized that it would please both my parents and God if I became involved in ministry. After all, I had been raised on the idea that serving God in full-time ministry was the epitome of finding purpose.

It was the mid '80s, when the explosion of TV ministries and the commercialization of contemporary Christian music were the driving force influencing us all. The appeal of television media was a relatively new vehicle for church ministries and what nearly every Bible college student aspired to attain. This was more hip and modern than my grandparents' tent meetings. It was fast-paced and high tech with unlimited potential for global reach. It made perfect sense.

During my time in Bible college, I was invited to be a regular singer on KFCB, a Christian television station in the Bay Area. That's where I started learning about television production behind the scenes. Later, a man from my church recognized me from the *California Tonight* program and asked if he could introduce me to his nephew. He described him as a student at Christ For The Nations Institute and a singer/evangelist. This man sounded sincerely on fire for Jesus, so naturally I was intrigued and gave the man my phone number for his nephew to call.

Singing was still where I placed my identity, and the idea of following the path of my musical parents was appealing to me. Bible college was where I gained a deeper hunger for worship, but I still lacked maturity in my walk with the Lord. Having grown up in the Southern Baptist Church, I hadn't been introduced to the concept of being baptized in the Holy Spirit or the type of worship we experienced in the Assemblies of God and charismatic churches until the end of my teen years.

The biggest impact came through a Full Gospel Business Men's Fellowship International conference where I met Cheryl Prewitt, a former Miss America, and heard her testimony of a miracle healing. It was at the precipice of having won my very first pageant title that my family was introduced to the gifts of the Spirit. I had witnessed deep worship at home when I heard my mother pray, and I truly valued my heritage, but it wasn't until I experienced worshiping with my contemporaries that my understanding for things of the Spirit began to broaden.

Unfortunately, I interpreted unusual circumstances to be from God the way some people might welcome guidance from a horoscope or tarot cards. So on the night that the man's nephew called me, I was too preoccupied with interpreting it as a divine appointment to notice the subtle signs that should have caused me concern. I should have paid better attention, but my curiosity kept me in the game.

He informed me that he was no longer a student at CFNI, but that he was convinced he was going to have a mega ministry. He fixated solely on a prosperity gospel, which I was not at all familiar with. His message deeply contrasted with my focus, which was to minister authentically, but the gospel, as I understand it today, had not yet penetrated my own identity, so I barely recognized the concept of real ministry myself.

I was naive and unaware of the counterfeits that could exist in the world of public ministry, trusting that others had the same sincerity for the Lord that my family and my mother's family did. We can convince ourselves of anything when we really want something to be true, and my sophisticated denial system was stronger than my spiritual sense at that time.

I wrestled with the awkwardness of our initial phone conversation but avoided drawing any conclusions until he turned on the charm. Soon we arranged a meeting with my family. His persuasive humor and Southern charisma sounded like sweet words of affirmation that outweighed his lack of spiritual depth for me. My father was quick-witted and funny, so this was a familiar trait to me, and he also played a guitar like my father. It seemed like a match made in heaven.

It felt right at the time because I had nothing to base my criteria for love on other than my upbringing to serve the Lord with a pure heart and moral character. I was sure that our letters, phone calls, and quick visits were sufficient enough to know him in the course of what led to our engagement. It wasn't an official proposal on bended knee; we simply discussed where we saw ourselves in five years, and the conversation ended with a beautiful ring on my finger and a few months to plan a wedding. Again, I was floating on air because I felt desirable and valued.

On the morning of our wedding day, my maternal grandfather passed away. It affected me deeply because we were very close. In many ways, my grandfather had shown me more affirmation and tenderness than my father, who was not comfortable with emotional intimacy. He had lived with us during my teen years but had been suffering from the late stages of Alzheimer's disease. After the wedding my new husband and I had planned to drive my car to Carmel-by-the-Sea for our honeymoon, and I did my best to compartmentalize my grandfather's death so that our wedding night would not be overshadowed by the sad news.

It was both strange and exciting as we drove away from the wedding venue, watching dusty pink and silver balloons slowly rise above the horizon in the rear-view mirror. Both of us dressed in our best *Miami Vice* fashion, we thought we had the world in front of us. He was a Texas boy, so the route to the Northern California coastline did not come naturally to him, and I had lost the directions to the hotel in the chaos of the wedding and news of my grandfather's passing.

This was before cell phones and GPS, so when he realized our predicament, he panicked and began to yell at me. I flinched in disbelief as the sting of his rejection pierced my already fragile heart. As his anger and shouting began to escalate, I froze with fear. I was a nervous new bride about to consummate marriage with a man that suddenly felt like a complete stranger to me. Without warning, he slammed on the brakes and pulled the car over to the side of the road. It would not be the last time I was abruptly thrown out of a car, and as he drove away, my heart raced in utter shock and disbelief.

At that moment, I didn't know what to do. Why would he leave me like that? My parents had invested all their hard-earned money into making my wedding day beautiful, and over 200 guests had been there to celebrate just a few hours earlier. *This* was the day I had waited for, but it felt more like a nightmare. My mother was home grieving the loss of her father after working tirelessly on our wedding, and I was standing at a fork in the road—literally and figuratively. Awkwardly poised in my high-heeled shoes on a remote stretch of dirt and gravel, I wanted to pinch myself to wake from this bad dream, but it had only just begun.

I'm not sure how many minutes passed before he returned to pick me up, but I decided to chalk it all up to wedding jitters. I was really good at drowning my realities in an ocean of denial, so I apologized for losing the directions, got back into the car, and we went on our merry way. That was my first indication that something lurid was lingering just beneath the surface of his volatile temper.

Within three months of our wedding day, the physical violence began after I tearfully expressed concern over a situation at my new job. I needed a little encouragement due to some mean-spirited females who had made it their mission to bully me, but encouragement was not what I received. His mother had been visiting that week and was sleeping on the sofa just outside our bedroom door.

I was talking quietly about the situation, hoping to get some supportive advice, but his reaction wasn't a natural one. I had unintentionally triggered his rage again, striking a financial nerve as he assumed I might quit my job. Money was his idol, and I quickly ascertained his unhealthy attachment to wealth and power as a type of identity. If anything stood in the way of his monetary goals, he became threatened and angry.

Before I knew what had happened, I was gasping for air under the stranglehold of his hands around my neck. His mother must have heard the struggle because she began knocking loudly on our bedroom door and calling his name. He pinned me under his knees, immediately turning to yell, "Go back to bed!" I was devastated when she obeyed his orders and walked away, but the interruption created enough distraction to cause him to settle down and go to sleep.

From that day forward, I walked on eggshells around him. However, I inevitably continued to trigger his anger without even trying, and he always had a way of convincing me that it was my fault. I tried desperately to win his approval. Like a good little pageant girl, I adapted my persona to align with his goals. Before long I was working for a major radio station on the Gulf Coast of Texas, selling advertising and doing voice-over work.

Utilizing my formal training, I started modeling again for a local agency, landing TV commercials and spokesmodeling gigs along with catalog photography and fashion layouts. Seeing my face on kiosks in retail stores and television commercials made me feel a certain sense of momentary success, but under my carefully rehearsed confident smile was a broken heart and a terrified little girl. I was hiding the evidence of abuse behind a mask of counterfeit happiness and feeling disconnected from the faith and family I had grown up with.

Resourcefully, I put my sequined pageant gowns back to use when my husband suggested that we start entertaining as a musical duet for private corporate events. All that changed, however, when I was offered a recording contract and opportunity to move to Nashville, starting as the opening act for Charley Pride. The general manager of the country music station that I worked for had discovered my talent and, unbeknownst to me, pulled some strings with his music contacts there. They approached me with a once-in-a-lifetime opportunity, but my husband became depressed and malignant over their disinterest in promoting us as a duo. So I did what I believed to be the right thing, and I turned the opportunity down.

My mother always taught me to value marriage and family above fame or fortune, but I didn't really know what a fulfilling marriage was supposed to look or feel like. Living with abuse was like sleeping with a hand grenade and hoping you didn't pull the pin when you rolled over in bed. I knew I was lost at sea and at its mercy.

Not long afterward, I lost my job at the radio station due to poor sales. I was suffering from pretty low self-esteem and had never been fired from a job before. I had the dreadful task of delivering the news that evening when my husband came home from work. His job was also in sales, and he frequently spent his days entertaining clients in strip clubs and buying them expensive lunches.

I had grown numb existing within this empty lifestyle, living thousands of miles away from my family, and feeling profoundly alienated from my own identity. We had attended neighborhood churches on occasion where I hoped to find a glimmer of purpose, but I felt jaded and it was hard to integrate with the people there. As I nervously awaited his arrival that evening, I barely remembered the girl I once was or the faith I'd once held on to.

When he arrived home, I sheepishly told him that I had lost my job that afternoon. Hoping for mercy, my heart sank as he freaked out and began pacing the floor. My mind raced anxiously as I watched his temper escalate. I was weary in body, mind, and soul, and utterly exhausted from the humiliation of having been fired earlier in the day and generally living a lie to the outside world. Before I even knew what was happening, I was staring down the barrel of a cocked and loaded handgun. As the room began to spin, I wondered if I would live to take my next breath.

I could feel my blood go cold as my adrenaline levels kicked in, causing my limbs and face to go numb. Without skipping a beat, the survivor in me silently prayed, *God, let me live!* I looked him squarely in the eye, knowing exactly what I had to do. I assured him that I would go and get my job back the next day. He paused for a moment, still aiming the gun at my forehead, and then with a sudden slump of his shoulders, he lowered the gun and it was over.

I don't know if that was the first time he actually thought about killing me, but I do know he was capable, because he had threatened my life several times over. The very next day, I did return to the employer who had fired me and begged him to give me another chance at it. Doing so was humiliating, but somehow I was able to *sell it* because I knew my life depended on it. My employer said, "I can't believe I'm doing this but okay."

A couple weeks later I was told my husband had a job transfer and that we would be relocating to San Antonio. Due to the strain I was under, that news came as a huge relief, and the prospect of starting over in a new town seemed like a chance to get away from the nightmare I had been living. After settling in San Antonio for a few months, I discovered that I was eight weeks pregnant, and for the first time in my life, I had something special to live for!

I loved everything about my pregnancy, including the maternity clothes that my mother-in-law helped me acquire. She was someone I highly admired as she was always dressed impeccably and seemed to have it all together. She was sharp and beautiful, energetic and driven. In a strange way, I aspired to be like her because she was the pinnacle of strength and beauty in my husband's eyes.

She took me shopping at a discount store, and we purchased a cute summer wardrobe to take care of my needs with a July baby on the way. I had been hired as a property manager that year, and we lived in a lovely townhome surrounded by live oak trees and rolling hills. Life seemed to be getting better for us. He seemed happier and tried noticeably to be a better person for a while.

I had previously learned to hide my bruises with the right clothing because he was careful not to hit me in the face. That changed a few months into my pregnancy when I confronted him with the pornography and condoms I'd found in his briefcase. He busted my mouth hard enough to cause nerve damage in my lip for about a year. I learned from a dentist some years later that the trauma to my front tooth had caused it to die because of my pregnancy. The dentist explained how calcium in a pregnant woman's body goes mostly to the baby, and I remember crying with a broken heart when he had to extract the tooth and replace it with a bad imitation, forever altering my once feminine smile. It felt like I was losing the best parts of me one piece at a time.

During my pregnancy we were regular attendees of Cornerstone Church in San Antonio where I was growing rapidly under John Hagee's ministry. Undoubtedly, God ordered my steps to sing with their Southern gospel group, Exaltation, and what a joyful season that was in my life. I grew closer to God and my church family and finally felt I had purpose with a baby on the way. None of them knew anything about the abuse in my marriage, and I didn't want to rock the boat in terms of the favor I had found with them, so I kept it to myself.

Not long after my baby girl was born, my husband once again lost his job. I was heartbroken when he announced that we would be moving to live with his parents in Oklahoma. San Antonio had been good to me. I had made lifelong friendships there, but I had to say goodbye to them and to my church family. Compartmentalizing my domestic desires to decorate a nursery, I complied in order to adapt to the necessary changes. That season revealed a lot to me as we were shut in by a month-long ice storm, and the tensions of codependency mounted in my postpartum winter.

The following spring, my in-laws provided me with airline tickets to visit my family in California because it had been four months since they had seen my baby. When I returned home, I was informed that we needed to move immediately, and my husband asked me to call my parents in California in the hopes of staying with them. Jumping at the chance to be near them again, I did just that. We loaded our car to move across country to my hometown. We lived with my parents for a year, and I stopped probing about what happened in Oklahoma between him and his parents, but I knew it wasn't good. I didn't realize how much danger still lay ahead for me, only that I had mercy for the hurt little boy I believed my husband to be.

Finally we were able to get into a place of our own with the hopes of building our future, but shortly thereafter, while driving home one afternoon with our toddler in the backseat, he started getting agitated about something that shouldn't have been a big deal. I simply asked him to please calm down and not discuss it any further, but that set him off and he repeatedly punched me on the side of my head and my body so hard that the bone in my hand was broken from the force as I shielded myself from his painful blows.

He then pulled a loaded gun out of the middle console of our car and, again, held it straight to my head. By this time our little girl was screaming, and I was terrified for what might happen next. Somehow I managed to utter something that calmed the atmosphere and he put the gun away. After twenty-four hours I had to see our family doctor due to the severity of injury to my hand, and he scolded me sternly for not leaving my husband. I made excuses about how I triggered his anger, but the doctor retorted, "No woman deserves to be beaten. I don't care what she's done!"

A couple days later, our baby girl asked, "Daddy, why did you put a gun on Mommy's head?" As he viciously barked back at her, "Because your mother's a b... ," a light went on in my head. I realized he had no filter for the hurtful words he chose to use and that I was not the only one who would suffer from his abuse. My daughter was now next in line to be either a victim of verbal and emotional abuse or groomed to accept it as normal. What a painful moment of truth that was for me.

I did what I could have never done merely for myself. I realized I had to protect my child, so I waited for him to leave the house and then left a note for him along with my beautiful wedding ring, stating that I only wanted my freedom and our safety. I thought if I bargained by leaving every valuable possession behind, he wouldn't come after me, so I took only my baby girl and our clothes. I knew that I had to protect her from the kind of life we were living, and I would find a way to make it on my own.

There were many occasions throughout our marriage that resulted in physical violence and my utter humiliation. I never believed the abuse was okay—I just didn't know what to do about it. So I soldiered on while he and his family projected their unspoken message of superiority over me. This kept me on the defense instead of in a place of healthy confrontation. Looking back, I realize that this was a method of mind control to keep me from disturbing their family system and a perfect example of intimidation and manipulation at work. The Bible refers to this as "the sin of divination" (1 Samuel 15:23).

I have always shown great tenacity and dedication in marriage; sometimes to my own demise. Perhaps I got that from my mom. She had unwavering courage combined with religious performance, which didn't always serve her, but it kept her praying for us through those hard years. In the end, I believe her tendency to put everyone else's needs before her own contributed to her failing health. I now understand that all the sincerity in the world will not save us from whatever we allow to remain broken and unhealed in our identity, regardless of which end of the spectrum our imbalance lies.

The patience of God is so poignant as He gently pulls the bandages off one layer at a time to cleanse our wounds with the truth of His Word, applying healing salve to the critical places that need transforming. He does not rush us in the process. Instead, He forbears and guards each step of our deliverance from generation to generation and from glory to glory. The only participation required is our surrender. We must trust Him with our deepest vulnerabilities and from every fiber of our being.

It took me another two years from the day I left my husband to finally muster the courage to file for divorce because of my religious bondage and concern for my Christian reputation. It was the strong counsel from a licensed professional (who was also a local pastor) that convinced me I was still in a lot of danger. He had previously counseled my husband and knew about his personality disorders. Sure enough, during the months that followed my petition for divorce, my husband stalked me repeatedly, showed up at odd times of the day and night, verbally threatening to take my life, and called me in the wee hours and on the job to harass me.

Thankfully, God provided a place of refuge during that dangerous time with a Christian family in Fresno who had known me since my pageant days. They offered a temporary safe haven for my daughter and me and were kind enough to make us feel at home. I'm convinced it was divine intervention that caught the attention of one of his friends who overheard his raging threats toward me, and together with his parents, finally pulled him away from California for good.

I had to live on government assistance for a while as a single mom to make ends meet while I studied for my real estate license. I had been hired to work as a mortgage loan officer, having no clue of what I really wanted in life. I simply needed to survive. Smiling on the outside, I was an emotional train wreck on the inside, barely managing my own condition let alone that of a strong-willed two-year-old who was now dealing with the absence of her father. I needed God's help like I had never needed it before, and I found Him to be ever present and faithful in my bed of pain. Just as Psalm 139:8 (GW) reads, "If I make my bed in hell, you are there."

I did not hate my daughter's father; I hated what he did. By God's grace, I was eventually able to forgive him. It required turning all of my painful regrets over to God and letting go so that I could forgive the wounds that had come from a wounded person indeed. I had great compassion knowing that he was also broken, but I had to recognize where my own perverted mercy had led me to live under demonic tyranny for too long.

I knew that if I was going to model a healthier example of love for my little girl, I had to make a clean break to survive on every level. For the first time in my life, I was released from trying to save my husband, and I learned to establish standards of good and bad behavior and stick to my boundaries no matter what the consequence might be. I know God loves him, and that enables me to keep some compassion for him. My prayer is that he too might allow truth and love to bring healing and freedom from the demons that have haunted him.

3

Destiny Beckons

It brings me to tears when I think of how God preserved my life against the enemy's plans to destroy me in the abuse of my first marriage. Jesus is often likened to a faithful shepherd who will leave the ninety-nine to go after the one who has gone astray. I've heard that a shepherd will slow down a runaway lamb by carrying it on his shoulders in order to retrain it to stay near him. The sheep then becomes familiar with the loving shepherd's voice and stays close to his abiding ear as its new-found intimacy causes the young lamb to recognize the dangers of its own propensity to run away. Faithfully, it will follow for the remainder of its life. Such was my case in the process of my surrender to God's ways.

I've often said that when God gave me a daughter, it saved my life because it awakened me to take care of us both. In some ways, she has always had better instincts for reading people than I ever did. She was a feisty child and keenly smart but was also deeply hurt by our fragmented home. I felt so much guilt about what she had been through, but I knew that it was up to me to stop the cycle of abuse and to model what love really looks like in a healthier way.

I gave her more freedom to voice her opinions than I had been given as a child because I wanted to encourage her to speak up and not be afraid to say no to bad people or destructive behaviors. This was tricky at times because I was also still learning how to find my own voice, and it often became a parenting riddle to figure out how to establish my loving authority while raising a strong-willed child who could outsmart me much of the time.

I'd been working in the mortgage field for a while and receiving government assistance for food stamps and medical aid, etc. Reporting to the department of social services always felt like I'd been reduced to just another number. No one cared about the variety of sad circumstances attached to any particular person standing in line, and to be honest, I wondered if any of them cared about each other. The state of California did care, however, about getting their reimbursement from my daughter's birth father, which required me to provide them with his address. However, I wasn't sure where he was living at this point, and I didn't want to know.

For fear of being stalked again, I decided not to pursue him and to terminate all government assistance because the risk far outweighed the benefits for me. We had been living without child support or spousal support since the beginning, aside of a couple random donations during our separation, as there had been no judgment against him in our divorce decree. I could only afford a paralegal to file my papers after a lawyer friend pointed me in the right direction. Money wasn't my focus even though, in hindsight, I probably should have been smarter about it. Fear was still driving me on so many levels, and all I cared about was that it felt safer to be on my own. It took some time to get past the trauma of the abuse and constant threats on my life, but I was willing to do whatever it took to stay alive.

By now I was turning thirty and wondering how my youth had vanished so quickly. Wanting to reclaim my life, I had a lot of sorting and managing to do but hadn't developed my organizational skills very well. My dream of singing wasn't exactly going to help me at this point, but

I practiced my faith in God to provide for my daughter and me as I applied my best efforts to succeed. It became a habit when my daughter needed something that I couldn't afford to take it to her heavenly Father, saying for example, "Your daughter needs a new coat!"

I knew that in His Word He had promised to be a Father to the fatherless and, without fail, God always provided for every single need that we had. I was always so grateful to Him for loving us that way, and I now recognize how He also loved me enough to stretch me and discipline me for a greater purpose. He didn't coddle me; He helped me grow in the necessary areas that I thought were shut down and incapable.

One year I had very little money for back-to-school clothes, and after asking the Lord to provide, I stumbled upon a yard sale where the sellers had just put out some *gently used* designer clothes in her exact size! I couldn't believe my eyes—the prettiest brand-name clothing in practically new condition. These were things I desired to buy for my little girl but could never afford to. I probably loaded fifteen bags of clothing into my car that day for pennies on the dollar. We usually shopped for everything at Walmart, and she especially loved the red and gold glitter shoes that they sold there. She wore them nearly everywhere, and it was apparent that she inherited my love of sparkly things. Not the same with the pageant bug, however, and I was quite grateful for that.

Oh how I loved her precious little heart. She was the center of my universe, and I wanted to teach her how to avoid the mistakes and pitfalls I had made, but this required my own healing on a foundational level, and I was still bound and gagged with a hijacked identity. For four and a half years I floundered between hope and shame, feeling that I was damaged or tainted for having been divorced. It took a while to get used to my self-perceived scarlet letter, and I longed to be in a secure relationship where I felt loved and protected.

I felt guilty and inadequate for not having a father figure for my little girl. This crack was a deep one and perhaps linked to my own daddy issues. So instead of finding contentment and satisfaction in our place in the journey, I began to ask God to send me a husband who would be a good father in our lives. I was unaware of the depth of my own wounds and that I was asking for something I was not ready for.

My vulnerability to believe in a broken concept of love also led me to accept some so-called prophetic words of knowledge that came from total strangers. Beware of these kinds of things when you have a personal agenda. The enemy can use them to derail you and make you think they are from God when God might actually be requiring you to *wait*. There were several unsolicited *words* about how I was going to meet a man, and one of these people said a new man would consider my daughter to be a bonus in our relationship. I was told that he would call her his little princess, and I wanted nothing more than that for her. Once again, I decided to interpret these prophecies to my own liking, and after four and a half years of single parenting, I met another man I wasn't necessarily attracted to but seemed safe.

I had recently been medically diagnosed with post-traumatic stress, which most likely started in my childhood. Having also experienced a marriage filled with violent anger and abuse, the feeling of safety was invaluable to me. I couldn't see much past that need. This new man was extremely quiet and seemingly humble in contrast to the braggadocio arrogance of my first husband. He was faithful in his church attendance and by all appearances, a gentle soul. I ignored some red flags while dating him, thinking that I was being too proud about my personal standards, but I now realize wisdom was lost on me.

I followed through with the relationship and married him three months later, blissfully ignorant of what I was jumping into but trying to mold it into my own ideal. It is said that still water runs deep, and that can be a double-edged sword. That was certainly the case in this situation, and oh how I wish I could get those years back. The water I was about to dive headfirst into was dark and stagnant, full of tormenting things that I could not see from its calm surface above. I had gone from bad to worse and nearly drowned in the bottomless pit of his control and mental abuse, but it was here that I learned how to swim.

We were married for ten challenging years that kept me reeling in confusion as I worked so hard at tenaciously loving him. I gave everything I had to happily nurturing our family and helping to raise his sons. But beneath the gentle façade, which he projected to the outside world, danger was lurking in the shadows of terrifying mental illness and extreme paranoia. I felt like small prey as the light of my own soul slowly dimmed under the control of his condemning accusations and verbal assaults. He was tormented by his own fears, and his paranoia convinced him that our neighbors, my doctors, and random acquaintances were either lusting after me or, worse yet, having affairs with me. He constantly berated me about my clothing, and although I was wearing baggy clothes to meet his approval, he had a way of making me feel dirty and guilty for being a woman.

I remember a day when time almost stood still for a moment on a rare outing with my mother. She pulled me aside at a clothing store and reached for a pretty handbag that was hanging on a nearby rack. It featured a picture of a girl's pink tulle skirt dangling over her pretty dancing feet, which were fitted with dainty high heels. Her eyes filled with tears as she said, "Baby, there is still a princess deep inside of you that needs to come back out and live! Don't lose yourself." She was able to see what I could not see, and from a mother's heart she not only pleaded with me to awaken but also covered us in prayer.

After eight years of succumbing to his very odd behaviors and beliefs, bearing the guilt he placed on me for just being a woman, and laboring hard to build a painting business that I could be proud of, I was like the frog in the kettle of water over a fire without the sense to jump out when it started to boil. When I did begin to awaken to the desire for a healthier me, I started self-nurturing again through weight loss and a more positive mental attitude. However, this caused him to feel threatened. Any sign of my femininity caused him to constantly berate me, whether it was about going to Weight Watchers meetings or wearing prettier clothes.

I was confused, hurt, and betrayed over the fact that he condemned me instead of cheering me on for my hard work. Meanwhile, he had been lusting over my best friend at the time, who had lost a considerable amount of weight and wore fun feminine clothing. He favored her when the three of us were together but would call her terrible names behind her back and tell me that I was going to be just like her. He would disappear from time to time, and I'd never know where he was. Once a couple days went by before he came home. It was as if he had an invisible wall around whatever he was protecting, and despite my efforts to penetrate this fortress, I was not allowed inside.

The last year and a half of our marriage became the most terrifying and mind-bending ordeal I have ever experienced as he manifested very dark, sexually themed hallucinations. He believed the neighbors were running brothels and scared me to death when he told me that the people living next door had infrared glasses and could see through our bedroom walls. I finally realized something much deeper than insecurity was going on when these hallucinations became a daily occurrence. Once I came home from work to discover that he'd bolted our bedroom door with four or five exterior fence locks from the inside. Night after night he placed booby traps beside my bed after I fell asleep so that I would trip on them if I got up in the night. He covered the windows with tinfoil, turning our beautiful home into a strange and unsafe place.

He began taking pictures of the houses adjacent to ours using his flip phone and a magnifying glass as if it were a zoom lens, convinced that he was capturing body parts in his photos. But when I looked at these so-called images, there was nothing but a black screen, and there was just no reasoning with him. Soon my worst potential nightmare came true when I realized he had also developed an unnatural affection toward my daughter. She had just turned fifteen, and I was highly concerned by the level of his sickness but was uninformed about what to do, frozen in my confusion. This just couldn't be happening, but it was.

I was plagued with thoughts about my vow to be faithful for better or for worse and felt the responsibility to fight for what was right, but understanding what was right had become allusive to me. Hoping that our licensed family counselor might help us find a breakthrough, I called her during a long episode of hallucinations one evening. She immediately came over to witness his behaviors for herself, and after nearly two hours of observation, she and I stepped outside to recap. As I walked her to her car, I clung to the sheer hope that she could help us fix whatever was wrong. Instead she shook her head no with eyes as big as saucers and told me there was something dreadfully wrong. There was no quick cure, and she was highly concerned, telling me that she could not give me any positive news on the prognosis.

She referred me to a psychiatrist in a neighboring town, and I made an appointment to see him. To convince my husband to go, I had to portray the visit as a source of help for me related to improving our marriage. After consulting with us about the issues of paranoia, the psychiatrist wanted to prescribe medication for him along with further treatment and observation, but he refused to return for the help he needed, saying that I was the one with the problem.

Every day grew increasingly unsafe as his paranoia and raging accusations intensified. He had a stout frame and a strong and muscular build, and as his gentle demeanor changed into an angry one, I knew he could easily hurt me. However, we loved him and cared about his well-being, so I prayed for his healing and anointed his pillow with oil, along with every doorpost of our home. Once again, I was weary from carrying the burden alone and protecting his reputation while also working on my interior design business.

My mother, who knew only a little about our situation, had already begun to sense that something was dreadfully wrong and expressed concern about my daughter's safety. She told me that she was starting an intentional time of fasting and prayer, asking God to expose whatever harm might be intended over my life and my daughter's. If there was one thing I could always count on, it was that God answered my mother's prayers!

The very next afternoon, we got our answer. My husband had broken into my daughter's bathroom by picking the lock on the door while she took a shower and then hid behind the shower curtain to watch her. When she realized that he was there, she screamed in horror and he recoiled, quickly leaving the room. I was on my way to work that day when I answered my phone to hear my daughter screaming, crying, and barely catching her breath. She was completely shaken to the point of hyperventilating, and I knew something devastating had happened. I immediately turned my car around to go rescue her, knowing we could not go on like this anymore. God had exposed a major deal breaker in my marriage and a way for our safe escape from a very close call.

The following day I received a phone call from Child Protective Services asking if I had taken my minor child from the home where the incident took place or whether she was still endangered. Apparently our family counselor was under legal obligation to report the incident after I called her, and they explained to me that if I had not removed her from the home, they would have come and taken her from my custody. It was a confirmation that brought me peace that I had done the right thing, and the Lord was merciful in His protection over us both. I could almost hear the sound of a slamming door closing out that decade of our lives.

Confused and worn out from the mind-bending roller coaster we had been on for so long, I questioned God about why He had allowed me to end up in such a terrible situation again. In the Bible, Jesus refers to an "evil and adulterous generation" who seeks after signs and wonders. He warns us that we should understand the signs of the times and be faithful to the Lord in that season. *Demanding* a sign is quite different from *knowing* the signs, and the only sign He says we will receive, in that case, is the sign of Jonah, who was swallowed by a large fish and remained there for three days (Matthew 16:4).

This picture points to the finished work of Christ, who remained in a tomb for three days before He arose to bring us new life. God had proven his faithfulness to me time and time again, yet I had wanted to rush His process of healing and restoration in the area of love, not realizing His love for me was enough. Instead of basing my decisions on the signs around me and the prophecies that sounded so good, I should have followed the advice of 1 Thessalonians 5:21 (NKJV): "Test all things; hold fast what is good." God's plan for me was good all along, but I was impatient. In my ignorance, immaturity, and lack of identity, I *demanded* a sign, giving credence to an inaccurate word that did not come from Him.

God allowed me to follow my own deception, patiently standing by while I processed in the belly of a beast for another season. It was a very dark grave for my soul, and I knew it would require a resurrection to revive it. Looking back, I know that God was not being harsh or unmerciful to me. He was not punishing me for my folly. On the contrary, it *was* His mercy that reached into the abyss, corrected the imbalance of my fragmented soul, and tore down the idol of human love and codependency.

My need for acceptance had stolen my genuine sense of worship that I had developed in my childhood. Whenever we are invaded or driven by a dangerous desire or false need that surpasses our need for God, we can be assured that it is an idol no matter how innocent it looks. But the mercy of Jesus remained with me through the process of my undoing and tearing down this false god by teaching me about His love. What felt like my death was, in actuality, my salvation.

There I was in the aftermath of the storm, feeling as if I had been washed up on the shore, freshly regurgitated from the belly of a whale. I did not understand yet why my life had become so broken despite all of my good intentions. I spent the next few days wailing into my pillow every night with a shattered heart, questioning how I had missed God again in this area of my life. I was no stranger to hearing His voice, but I can look back now and recognize exactly where I didn't have total peace in either of my marriages, and I chose to overlook that still, small voice that would have led me to divine wisdom. God was so present in my life, but there were unredeemed areas and mindsets that I chose to spiritualize instead of change.

I had demanded all the signs from God that would piece my life back into the order that I wanted it to be, and the only sign I was left with was the sign of Jonah. What a hard way to learn such a lesson, but it was a valuable one nonetheless. It was time to give God all the messy pieces of my shattered attempts at happiness and trust Him completely to be my faithful provider and healer no matter how long it might take. I did not deserve His restoration, but His mercies proved new to me every morning.

After a few months of living in a borrowed bedroom at my cousin's house, my head began to clear, and the Lord spoke to me about my daughter and me relocating. She had been through so many traumas that it had finally taken a tremendous toll on her. I was gun-shy about trusting whether I was hearing from God at this point, so I asked Him to confirm it at least three times. I did not want to make another huge mistake. God was good to me and He did confirm His direction for us to move to Dallas three different ways. At that point I obeyed.

Sometimes God does give us signs, but those signs must align with His Word! He will never tell us to do something contrary to His Word, and we will always have peace when it is God. I hadn't felt peace like that in years, and not only did He confirm His direction, but He also made huge provisions to make it happen. In the process of my obedience and realignment to His Word and His will, another huge prayer was also answered. My teeth, which had been damaged by my first husband, were beautifully restored. The smile that I once cried over being destroyed was suddenly better than it had ever been before. The resources we needed for moving to Dallas also became available when we agreed to sign off the deed to our house.

I had loved that house from the beginning of its foundation, having used my talents and hard work to paint, finish, and furnish it. But a house is not a home without the safety and love that it's intended to hold. I was able to take a portion of the equity and some of the smaller furniture, which provided the immediate funds necessary to move. It felt as though we were walking on red carpet while God ordered every step ahead of us. It truly was a miracle for that kind of provision to take place without months of litigation and lawyers getting involved. God had made a way where there seemed to be no way!

There was one final test that I would have to pass in order to see my blessings fully manifest, however. I had been working on a commercial redesign for a friend who owned a retail jewelry establishment and committed myself to finish the work there before I left town. In the course of three months I had become emotionally attached to the friend who was so kind and compassionate toward my situation. He was handsome and well respected in the community. While my heart felt weak for the love and attention I seemed to be getting after years of control and trauma, I knew in my Spirit that it was a distraction from what God had already directed me to do.

Sometimes good things can be the enemy of God things! As difficult as it was, I turned down a proposal to stay in my hometown where I could marry a sweet, successful man, and I chose to obey what the Lord had told me to do. With my mama at my side, a new puppy, and two friends to drive the truck, we hit the open road. Like breath coming back into my lungs, I felt joy slowly but surely penetrate every part of my being. As scenes of the colorful Arizona terrain, with its tall pines and cacti, gave way to the sunsets of New Mexico, I drank it up like therapeutic medicine. We were headed toward a new horizon where destiny beckoned me like a beautiful song coming from my radio.

4

|||||||||||||||||||||||||||||

Coming Out of the Chrysalis

My sister lived in the Dallas area, and I was excited for the opportunity to be close to her again, as the years and miles had caused us to drift apart. Circumstances beyond our control, however, delayed the progress of restoring our relationship when she too was thrown into survival mode. Unable to be much more than a loving support to one another, we pressed on. I did everything I could to think ahead and build a new life for my daughter. We were well on our way to integrating our California roots into a Texas lifestyle.

After about a year of living in a North Dallas suburb, my daughter was happily enrolled in a private Christian school where she was a varsity cheerleader. We seemed to have made it over the hump so to speak. She had met the sweetest young man at church who truly loved Jesus and was a darling ray of sunshine to everyone who knew him. He was older than her, but he was very respectful and came from a very large, precious family. His daddy was a Gospel Music Hall of Famer, and he shared his father's gift of musical composition and playing piano.

I had prayed quite a lot over my concerns for my daughter with all she'd been through and wanted her to have something better than what I had experienced in my life. Watching her happiness made me feel like my prayers had been answered. It was a breath of fresh air. Her boyfriend was the type of guy who would share Jesus with a stranger and help anyone in need. He was such an encouraging example to my daughter as she grew in her relationship with the Lord. I witnessed her heart go from a tight little bud to a rose in full bloom. It was as if sunshine and laughter had come back into our lives again and things were starting to feel like they made sense.

Then the tide turned and everything rapidly changed. On an ordinary day like any other I was on my way to the grocery store when I had a very strange vision while driving my car. It was as if a movie played on a screen in my mind's eye, and I saw myself answering a phone call. The voice on the other end was the best friend of my daughter's boyfriend delivering the news that he had been hit and killed by a vehicle while riding his motorcycle. In this vision we rushed to the scene of the accident where pandemonium played out like an episode of *The Twilight Zone*.

Immediately I rebuked the thought and prayed a quick, but intentional, prayer of protection over him, putting fear out of my mind. It was only two weeks later that it actually came to pass, and we were devastated. Word for word, his best friend repeated what I had seen and heard in my vision, and I felt as if I were dreaming. Hearts racing in disbelief, my daughter and I rushed to the scene less than two miles from our home. We had just been with him earlier that morning.

The previous week had been filled with so much joy and laughter as they both had asked me for my blessing over their plans to be married some day. Paramedics and police cars were blocking the road as I pulled my SUV into an open field where my sister and nieces stood waiting for us. It was an extremely hot August day as we ran across the paved intersection, praying that he was still alive. Trying to catch our breaths in the heavy Texas heat, we learned from onlookers and acquaintances that the driver of a rock hauler truck had run a red light in a highway construction zone, and our beloved friend, who had become more like family to us, was struck while proceeding through the intersection.

As paramedics and officers slowly began to move aside, we could see that a tarp had been placed over his body, revealing only his boots. With a loud gasp, my daughter's knees buckled under the sudden shock, and she crumbled to the ground with a guttural cry. Just then, that hot August day turned ice-cold when an insensitive officer who was trying to clear the crowds impatiently yelled at us to leave the area. As I tried to explain who we were to the victim, he shouted at us, "Yes, he's gone!" We scrambled to obey him, but the shock was there to stay.

The strangest irony was that we had just attended his father's memorial service the week before after he'd lost his battle with cancer. The boy's poor mother had been through so much loss in such a concentrated amount of time. It was all just so surreal. Understandably overcome with grief, his mother asked us if we would go to the morgue in her place to claim his personal effects later in the evening. Still spinning in disbelief, we went to the morgue and they allowed us to see him in a separate room where we prayed over his body in the hopes of witnessing a miracle of resurrection. That miracle did not come the way we wanted it to, but we continued to hold on to our trust in Jesus.

It was almost unbearable to accept what we could see with our eyes. Our hearts could not make sense of it. My heart broke like never before as I witnessed my daughter manage things well beyond her years as she said goodbye to what she thought was her future. With huge tears trickling down her sweet face, she bent down to kiss him on his forehead, softly whispering, "I'll see you in heaven ... I love you."

The days and months ahead were the hardest yet to face. I felt like a failure as a mother, my daughter was grieving more than her fair share of trauma at the tender age of seventeen, and I was barely learning to make it on my own again. I could not afford to let my focus falter. Once again, I was shaken to my core, and I had to figure a way out of the overwhelming throes of my own pain in order to facilitate continued healing for us both.

It is so much harder to watch your child hurt than it is to be hurt yourself. When they're little you can bandage their cuts and soothe their bruises, but there's a helpless feeling when a parent cannot absorb the painful emotional trauma that life can throw at them as young adults. A tremendous sense of guilt creeps into your soul when you cannot fix it. This is the place where I found Jesus to be more real to me than ever before. I didn't need my mother's version of Jesus or anyone else's. I needed my own revelation of who He is in the deepest, darkest pit of our pain.

Cognitively I knew that He loved my baby girl even more than I did, and while the loss was significant to everyone who loved this beautiful young man on so many different levels, God's faithfulness would remain close to us all. After everything that we had endured, I didn't have much to give to anyone other than words of encouragement. But from my own quiet place, I prayed that God would carry us all where no other human possibly could.

During this time, we really had no roots in a church family that knew us well, and only a handful of new friends and acquaintances. My life-line of hope became Christian television. I hungered after God's Word to give me sustenance when I needed strength and faith to believe He had not forgotten us. The richness of His mercy came through great teachers who delivered anointed truth to me in my dark little cocoon. I was spiritually and emotionally pulverized, and whatever joy I had gained was now eaten up by grief. I was confused and questioned everything I believed in. But God had placed something supernatural in my DNA that would transform me from the inside out to manifest His brilliant image in my resurrected life.

Life had humbled me considerably since my pageant days, and I would have traded a million crowns if they could replace what had been stolen, damaged, or lost on my journey. I was growing much closer to Jesus as I spent time in His life-giving Word and was so far past the superficial longings of this world. Caught between my past and my future, I faintly remembered how I once longed to be someone special by the world's definition. I couldn't have anticipated how deeply painful my journey would have to be to help me discover what made me special. It was in the unraveling of my self-made persona that Jesus gave me the crown of life and taught me how to fly.

I began to understand how God molds us on His potter's wheel, precisely rebalancing our self-perceived importance. This painful, but critical, process slowly centers us just like a mass of clay before it is penetrated and shaped.

In other words, God sees the imperfections beneath the surface of our existence, and He deliberately corrects our imbalances, removing those unusable elements that would weaken the integrity of our vessel. The process usually feels like starting all over again, but our painful experiences are the reset button that brings our focus back to Christ, the solid rock, so He can reshape us and raise us up for His originally intended purpose.

I'm in no way suggesting that God brings evil things into our lives to shape us. Most usually those things come through the doors we have left open as the result of our own deception or ignorance, but His mercy reaches in to preserve us from total destruction and help us navigate our way out. We also know that rain falls "on the just and on the unjust" (Matthew 5:45 NKJV), but when those storms come, there is a promise for every child of God to hold on to. If you love the Lord and are called according to His purpose, He will work all things together for your good (Romans 8:28).

I like to refer to my time in Dallas as the season that God strengthened me and hardened me to difficulties, just as the Bible tells us He will in Isaiah 41. I call it my Ruth journey because I gleaned at the corners and edges of the fields I had been placed in. In that season, God provided miracle after miracle to strengthen me, and I learned to trust Him completely as my husband and provider. He was my comforter and the lover of my soul. I fell in love with Jesus and worshiped Him from the core of my existence and through everything I put my hands to do.

In a world of wolves dressed like sheep, I chose to place my trust in Him alone. This was the time for me to gain wisdom and understanding, as well as discerning of spirits, when dealing with people on every front—especially men. After a couple years of working for a talent agency as well as a bank, I decided to pursue interior design full-time again. It hadn't been my first career choice because walking away from the business I had built with my blood, sweat, and tears in California when I escaped my second marriage had been devastating. I was afraid that I had used up all my creativity and felt like a burned-out little fish in a giant ocean. There were design firms on nearly every corner that could either help advance me or hinder me. I knew that I would not succeed without God's favor, and I prayed heavily over my decision.

It was obvious how deeply my daughter was spiraling in grief, and I realized the importance of being available for her. As a single mom I needed the flexible work hours and better income potential that design work could provide, but it was a huge leap of faith for me. I knew from experience that entrepreneurship would be hard work but potentially rewarding. I adjusted the rates I had grown accustomed to charging in order to prove myself in a new market. What really impacted me was how timely and faithful God always was about answering my specific prayers and needs.

The deadline of my decision had arrived when my phone rang and a very sweet lady said she'd received my name from a Christian friend who knew that I was a designer. It was my moment to take the reins and not look back. I was partially a self-taught designer with some formal training through online courses and experience working in furniture gallery showrooms, but my biggest challenge was the administrative side of things.

Creatively speaking, I had no fear, and my painting skills, as a former decorative artist, would come in handy once again when I was asked to finish walls and cabinets. As word got out about the quality of my work, my clientele grew quickly. Dallas was a large metroplex with a small town vibe for hospitality and tightly knit communities, which turned out to be the perfect place to thrive. God knew exactly where to position me for my next level of training and development.

I remember many days when my body ached from the labor of working alone, but I was determined to not give in to a victim mentality. Pressing through my pain was only possible by giving praise, as my joy in the Lord truly became my strength. I found great favor among the elite circles of Dallas–Fort Worth where eventually my painting projects segued into designing entire homes and commercial spaces, raising my income potential through the sale of furniture and textiles.

My talent for design and my confidence grew as God ordered my steps. Eventually I was provided the opportunity to work under contract for a major corporation with government affiliation, doing commercial design for their corporate offices as well as their executive suite in the Texas Rangers stadium. I was much like the young ruddy-faced David in the Bible before he became a king. Anointed for something more than where I had been or where I was, but faithfully tending to the sheep in my pasture when the urgency of facing my own Goliath suddenly came upon me. I truly believed that with God, I could break every chain and do anything He appointed me to do!

Dating was not my biggest priority, although I did believe that God didn't intend to keep me single forever. I had learned that instead of trusting my old instincts, I needed to weigh every situation before the Lord and follow His leading. My natural propensity was to fall too hard, too fast. I was tested on this but thankfully passed each and every one until I became quite contented to be on my own.

I asked the Lord to straighten out my crooked paths and reveal what had caused me to end up a victim of domestic abuse twice with a trail of broken wreckage that probed at my underlying shame. I had never seen my father physically abuse my mother, although the dynamics of emotional abuse were normal in my growing-up years, so it took some time for me to recognize those behaviors as wrong.

I found the following details from an article published online by the Energetics Institute about the impact of child sexual abuse to be very compelling. Due to the deep trauma at work in a survivor's situation, adults will have one of two postures toward life after such abuse; they will either collapse or they will attempt to rise above the abuse. Some are unable to function in one or more areas of their life, often depressive or addictive, with a victim persona. Others dissociate from the trauma, soldiering on, but withdraw from or feel impaired by intimate relationships.

Love is a key dependency need of the child who will endure the abuse for even a scrap of love in return. Self-justification later results in abusive and destructive relationships where the adult abuse survivor stays in abusive relationships, minimizing the abuse and fixating on a sense that they are really loved by the abuser. This is why they forgive and re-enter the same destructive cycles. It's reported as "battered partner syndrome." Having been forced to bond traumatically to the parent who represents both "good parent" and "bad parent" often forces a split in the child's own identity. As "good" and "bad" are internalized, an unconscious fear develops that if one were to let go of the "bad parent" then one would lose the "good parent" too.[1]

When I read this article, it was like looking into a mirror for the first time and recognizing the origin of my own identity: split and fractured memories. It was actually quite comforting to finally understand the motivation behind my behavior patterns. For the sake of burying my trauma, I also internalized the good and the bad as inseparable, which caused me to be conflicted about who I was in my relationship with God. This kept me in abusive relationships for far too long, always thinking I should forgive the abuser or even accept blame because they *gave me love*, and love is what I longed for most. I had learned unhealthy boundaries from both sides of my immediate and extended family, and I was double-minded in many ways.

It has taken me years to adopt healthier ways of thinking, but I did it with God's help and wise counsel that I sought out along the way. It's important to understand that as you initially begin to change old mind-sets you will feel very raw due to the unfamiliarity of the process. That is why the time we spend in God's Word, prayer, and praise is so valuable to reshaping the construct of our inner selves. Subsequently, the time and energy spent intentionally changing our external habits and patterns are the key to fully establishing an identity in Christ.

Building new habits helps you quickly realize that you don't have to exist in a state of perpetual death any longer. Where once you were like a valley of dry bones, Jesus speaks life into your impossibility (see Ezekiel 37). It's a progressive and steady work where the sinew, muscle, and flesh begin to take form, and the breath of life awakens you to new strength until suddenly and purposefully, you can see how He has clothed you with His armor. There is nothing more validating or beautiful than to realize that you've become a mighty warrior, ready for battle against the enemy's lies, and nothing can stop you from your purpose as a purveyor of the message of hope for someone else.

During those years of rebuilding God's way, my daughter met another handsome man and was ready to embark on her own journey. They were married in a small ceremony and I suddenly had an empty nest. It was a time in my life to fight the right fight and move past the things that had nearly destroyed me. Regardless of those who had hurt me in my past, God's grace was sufficient to uniquely and effectively bring me to a peaceful place of forgiveness where I learned to quit focusing on my pain. I learned to be a giver and not a taker. When I desired friends, I learned how to become one to others. When I needed provision, I happily donated my money, time, or things that I owned to bless someone else who was in need.

The law of reciprocity is a lot like planting seeds in every area of our lives, and I found the adventure with God to be thrilling! He taught me how to love without strings attached, focusing on giving from a place of strength instead of neediness, and it changed me completely. I became much more useful for His kingdom in my ordinary circumstances, and as I applied this same principle to the hope of restoring true love, I not only became the kind of friend to others that I would personally want to have, but I also thought about what type of man I would like to marry one day. I knew that I had to become the same type of person in character that I wanted to attract. Cheerfully, I gleaned like Ruth from the fruit of my fields, waiting and trusting that in God's perfect time he would find me.

After five years in Dallas, I was not settling for anything less than what I knew God would want me to have in a relationship. I had dated a few nice guys, but I was no longer interested in merely finding companionship; I had already found tremendous companionship with Jesus. What I wanted was a life partner in love, ministry, and adventure who shared my goals and values. So when a guy didn't meet my criteria for true potential on a spiritual, emotional, or physical level, I didn't waste my time or theirs.

Little did I know that God was about use a musical acquaintance of mine to introduce me to the man who would change the trajectory of my life. I had grown accustomed to not truly being loved by human men, but I was finally satisfied by God's acceptance of me. I recall it was a sweet time when I focused on nurturing my own needs, buying my own flowers, and celebrating my life with beautiful music, candles, and elegant dinners that I made at home.

During the day I beautified multi-million dollar homes, but I was wonderfully smitten with my little apartment and its balcony view. I considered myself blessed to make a decent living with the talents God had given me, and I had an amazing plethora of faithful friends. Contributing my time and talents to a local church worship team also restored me to ministry. Life was not perfect, but it was oh so joyful.

I met Paul in the fall of 2009 when he was traveling through Dallas to Orlando for Thanksgiving. He and I had made a few exchanges on social media earlier that year via our mutual friend, and I thought nothing of it other than noticing he had a crazy funny sense of humor. When we met in person, he was very kind and so easy to talk to. It was such a refreshing change from the usual burden of having to carry on a meaningful conversation with someone who didn't contribute much. I didn't feel pressured to perform or judged only by my appearance. We laughed a lot and a real friendship formed between us.

I had grown used to men who were completely lacking in their passion for God try to wine and dine me with their schmoozy talk about careers and material wealth. I wanted to get to know Paul first and simply reciprocated his friendship. He was so different from all the others, and he also seemed genuinely interested in getting to know me. Wow, a man who actually wanted to learn about who I was on the inside—what a change!

It wasn't until our third date that something magical happened that completely shifted my perspective. I had just arrived for our date, and it was raining cats and dogs that night in Dallas. The white holiday lights were twinkling in all the trees that lined the shops, and the temperature had significantly cooled—a welcome reprieve from the usual heat. I was still sitting in my car, patiently waiting my turn at the valet drop off when someone knocked on my passenger window.

It was Paul, perfectly silhouetted with his umbrella against the festive trees. As he leaned in to say hello, a closer look revealed his beautiful blue and white designer shirt with the fancy printed cuffs that I just adored. He was dashing and handsome, kind and considerate, awaiting my arrival like a gentleman, and it took my breath away! That sort of thing had never happened to me before in my life, and I'll always remember it as if it were yesterday. I still get chills remembering that moment.

Could it be that God Himself, planted something special in my heart that night? I believe He did and that He let me see Paul for who he really was, on the whole. Later that evening, he held my hand for the first time as we watched a movie, and it felt as if he were holding my heart instead. I'm sure that probably sounds too corny to be true, but it was significant to me, as I'd never felt that way before. A few more months passed before we shared our first kiss on the San Antonio River Walk. That was the night when I knew that I could grow to love this man forever.

The potential for real love had suddenly become tangible and, without a doubt, God was at the center of this new relationship.

When certain things are authored by God, they require our partnership with Him to obtain them. Such was the case with our marriage. There were a lot of other circumstances that made our relationship difficult and even worked it from the beginning. I simply had to give it back to God and let Him handle it for me. I put it to the test, and time would tell whether it was truly His plan for us to be together beyond friendship.

In the meantime, I lived to the best of my ability, loving Paul from a distance through prayer. I chose to remain open about dating other people, but when I did date others, my love for Paul became more obvious. I realized that regardless of what these other guys had to offer me in terms of good looks, success, status, or money, none of them could hold a candle to what I felt with Paul. Being with him was truly like coming home.

During that time, God showed me how to hold on to love with an open palm instead of with a fist, helping me realize that fear would crush it. It was a season of testing that prepared us for what was yet to come. I now believe it was a vital part of equipping us both for His purposes as we've become battle hardened. While Paul had already proven that he valued me as a person, the flip side of that coin was that he required more from me than talent, beauty, or brains. He had a lot at stake since he was tied to the family empire of Trinity Broadcasting Network during that season of his life, and his keen ability to see beyond people's masks matched my own.

I too had a lot at stake with the trail of brokenness that was behind me. However, while I had developed proven character through hard work and faith, it was imperative that I allow God time to bring this tiny seed to harvest and embrace my strength and spiritual discernment during this season of waiting. I knew that if it was really God, nothing and no one could separate what He had put together.

Essentially, the obedient actions I applied to my unwavering trust in the Lord stood the test of time. My prayers for Paul were not petitions for a husband, but rather, prayers that covered him with the blood of Jesus to protect him from whatever the enemy had planned for his life. I also asked that if the Lord did not intend for me to be Paul's wife that He would send the right woman to love him like he had never been loved before. I knew better than to ask for my own agenda and simply trusted that God knew what I could not yet see.

After a year of no contact with one another I came to a decision, asking God to release me from praying for Paul if it was over. That evening I was ready to bury it in the past and wish him only happiness since the relationship seemed to have run its course. I waited in stillness that night and simply wanted peace, but God did not answer in a way that I was expecting. Instead of giving me closure, I heard the Sprit of the Lord say, "Read Habakkuk 2:3." This was a passage that I was not yet familiar with.

Unaware of what I would find, I opened my Bible and knew it was a turning point for me. God had provided me with the peace and confirmation I sought, and from that moment on, I simply believed. "For the revelation awaits an appointed time; it speaks to the end and will not prove false. Though it linger, wait for it; it will certainly come and will not delay."

Just days after my father passed away and four years after we first met, Paul returned to me a changed man, and I had changed for the better too. He had gone through a serious tragedy and shared from his heart about His love for the Lord and his family. We had both individually settled some things that previously prevented our relationship from moving forward, and we were now ready, knowing that we truly had a special love for one another and that God's mercy would shine through our former brokenness.

Beyond our flaws, we recognized the treasure buried deep within the soil of who we had become, and love's healing power had given us a second chance. A year and a half later, we were married in a small ceremony. Surrounded by our faithful friends and a few family members, I walked down a makeshift aisle between white folding chairs in a pale blush gown. As my sister sang the song from *Twilight*, "A Thousand Years," we both knew the significance of its meaning and the longevity of true love.

If you had asked me twenty or thirty years ago where I would be today, I would never have dreamed this to be the picture of my life or even the picture of restoration—and neither would Paul. For both of us, restoration has been progressive and still is. It has required hard work, but it has come through grace, forgiveness, and the willingness to continually be changed into God's image.

We are agents of healing to one another, and together we grow daily knowing that God has given us an undeserved chance at love, life, and ministry from the seeds of our heritage and the legacy of faith that precedes us both. His promises are true but never as easy as one, two, three, done! However, they are worth every sacrifice given in obedience to redeem them. Love isn't love until it has to be given away and laid down for the good of someone else.

5

||||||||||||||||||||||||||||

Faulty Foundations

The Governor

While drafting my own story of overcoming various levels of abuse, I was profoundly moved by the shock and regret I felt for not having changed my patterns much sooner. Looking back on the minutia of past mistakes from my current vantage point casts a drastic new perspective on how I used to think.

During my years of my domestic abuse, I was too deep in the forest to find my way out of its entangling trees. The mental struggles that victims of abuse must navigate are often tormenting and should never be downplayed. Proverbs 18:14 (NKJV) asks, "The spirit of a man can sustain him in sickness, but who can bear a broken spirit?" Because there were many areas of truth that I was blind to, I needed the firm yet gentle touch of Jesus taking my hand in His to lead me out into the light.

People often callously ask, "What makes women stay with abusers?" While there are many contributing factors to this complex answer, I can tell you that the root cause is a deceptive mindset that keeps a person trapped in the grip of abuse. What kept me returning to such an unhealthy lifestyle was my foundational identity of shame and religious performance that dictated my choices. This was the faulty foundation that had shaped my sense of self-worth and kept me disconnected from the truth that I so desperately wanted to believe.

Proverbs 26:11 speaks of how a fool will return to his folly like a dog returns to its vomit, and I can't think of a better visual description for a codependent person who vacillates between their need for healthier boundaries and their toleration of control and abuse in the struggle for self-worth. I didn't recognize my own foundational belief system to be the root of my problem when I was steeped in the stronghold of certain mindsets. It took the mercy of God to graciously awaken me and His healing process to empower me to break the chains that had held me so tightly in my personal prison.

The bedrock of your beliefs is the foundation on which your identity is based and the governing force that influences your every move. How you perceive yourself impacts how you live, how you love, and how you serve (or fail to serve) the people around you. This principle explains the narcissistic tendencies of our present culture and how self-absorbed people are, even in the church today. Let it serve as a reminder regarding our responsibility to awaken from our slumber and minister well to the next generation. These belief systems begin as early as childhood, and if they are not based on the truth of God's Word, they must be deconstructed before new ones can be constructed.

Understanding the truth of God's Word, however, requires more than simply reading and quoting it, which is what we've become so good at doing. Obviously God's Word is the beginning and end of our barometer for knowledge, but the true revelation of who you are will be revealed in the Word incarnate. Jesus Christ speaks to your whole person, body, soul, and spirit, and transforms you from glory to glory in a personal and intimate relationship.

You might parrot the truth about *who* you are and *whose* you are in your religious clichés and Sunday mantras, but pay close attention to the fears that tend to drive your focus and motivations—even in your good works. Are they incongruous with the words you're saying? If so, you don't really believe what you profess, regardless of how sincere you are. You must remove the veil from your face and become vulnerable with God in order to look into the mirror of His glory so that you can really know who you are (see 2 Corinthians 3:18).

There are hidden cracks or fault lines within the foundations of our natural identities, but a closer examination by the Master Builder, Jesus, reveals what can only be mended or restored by His grace. It's His love and mercy that are working together to expose those faults to us all, because He wants everyone to discover who they are in Him.

It's hardest to trust God if your trust has been broken by someone who should have protected you, and it's quite common to create inner vows for self-protection. These are not always intentional acts of rebellion toward God, but they can be spiritual transactions against His will for us. They are sacred covenants that sound something like this: *I won't allow anyone to come close enough to hurt me ever again. I will unleash vengeance on those who have betrayed me. I can't trust anyone but myself.* These vows may seem like the only solution to your pain, but they are actually suggestions from the enemy, sent to dissuade you from the truth of God's love and govern you with a lie.

Inner vows work like a hook in the jaw to carry your focus away from Jesus as your total source of life and identity, which causes you to become the guardian and protector over your own life, and that is too big a burden for any of us to carry. I'm not referring to the assignment of stewarding over your life or absolving your partnership responsibility. We were all created to take dominion over the earth and do our part here. But if we surrender to our wounds instead of identifying with our God, we are rendered powerless.

Those who have been hurt at the most fundamental levels are often unaware when they have been derailed, bound, and gagged spiritually or emotionally by their wounds because, outwardly, they appear to function just fine. However, individuals who have suffered from assaults against their identity often cope with their internal pain by *shutting down* in one way or another.

The effort to avoid being hurt again can leave some isolated and coasting through life on emotional and spiritual autopilot, never really knowing how to engage authentically in relationships. This will sabotage every aspect of life. My respected friend Dr. Mark Chironna has said, "Everyone needs to have a sense of belonging. It takes two to know one."[2] The latter sentiment is a quote from the late anthropologist Gregory Bateson that reminds us we cannot know ourselves by ourselves. This hearkens back to God's original assessment when He was in Eden: "It is not good for the man to be alone" (Genesis 2:18).

According to the *Journal of Traumatic Stress*, some of the psychological effects of coping with sexual trauma include helplessness, rage, fear, loss, shame, and guilt.[3] These can have a debilitating impact on how we view and value everything in life and can only be rectified through healthy counsel and the healing and redeeming power of Jesus' blood. I am living proof that we can go from coping to thriving with the help of His daily renewal.

Recognizing the faulty foundations that have sabotaged your future doesn't usually come easy. This process requires the effective work of the Holy Spirit to peel back each layer as He gently steers you away from the trappings and mindsets that you've become so accustomed to. It can be messy and painful, but He is eager to help you when you call on Him and has promised that He will never leave or forsake you as you walk it out! Now this requires a choice on your part—that you will keep seeking Him, that you will not choose to forsake Him.

There's a tyrannical mindset that we're starting to see in our culture demanding that we comply with society's godless beliefs. Sadly, many believers have fallen prey to the influence of this deception, becoming apathetic in their pursuit of knowing Christ. The reciprocal relationship God intended for each of us is one that neither expects Him to do all the work for us or leave Him out of it entirely. We are partners in fellowship with His abiding love. It was the late theologian Augustine who said,

"To fall in love with God is the greatest romance; to seek Him the greatest adventure; to find Him, the greatest achievement."[4]

Without an awakening to and understanding of how personal wounds affect identities, some in the body of Christ will continue to be subject to their emotional constraints and powerless to recognize the difference between what appears to be good and what is godly. People mistakenly align with the god of culture because it appeals to their emotions and they are unable to discern a counterfeit Jesus when they see one. It's time to find your true voice by discovering yourself as God sees you.

The Great Impersonation

What God values most is His creation of mankind and our relationship to Him through worship. We were created in His image, and we're the temples in which He desires to dwell. But satan's infinite rage against God fuels his agenda to interrupt the dwelling place of God's glory, branding it with a different image. When our fellowship with God is hindered or broken, we are then distracted from our true source of identity and vulnerable to adopting a cheap imitation in its place.

My own journey led me to the bright lights of the stage, where glittery gowns and makeup were the tools I used to create a more loveable persona that made me feel special. I felt more loved and empowered when I sang and could hold an audience captive. The sound of their applause was like a pain pill when I needed to abandon my own self-rejection. I felt brave when I took the stage and believed anything was possible under those lights. It was my way of bettering myself, and for a while, God let me soar on that plane.

I was sincere in my pursuit of finding self-worth and even prayed that I would bring glory to God. I'm certain that He saw my desperate heart in the midst of my confusion, and He was faithful to walk me through every stage of my progress, even blessing me along the way. For years I continued to think of my persona as a genuine part of my identity, but there were some things that would have to be uncovered in order for me to move forward.

God used my painful journey to shake my protective mask loose and reveal how I had compensated for self-hatred and my fear of rejection. I slowly but surely realized how insufficient my coping mechanisms were and how my belief about myself was poisoning my good intentions, even in ministry. I had to get real about the intensity of my pain and stop running from my shame by allowing God into my most taboo places with some very honest dialogue.

I believe that when a person becomes broken in spirit outside of God's presence, they become spiritually vulnerable. The deceiver comes to manipulate and reinforce his cruel lies and plant a stake through the heart of their identity. This is especially true when it comes to child sexual abuse, and the stigma left behind can cause a person to lose sight of themselves. In today's narcissistic culture, it's common for people to hide behind the version of themselves that they project on social media or in social circles when they are actually isolated and alone.

When deception takes advantage of a wounded identity, the need for empowerment often has the potential to evolve into a lust for power by way of ungodly methods. Like a vampire who cannot see his own reflection, the insatiable appetite for love and approval turns inward and twists the beauty of our divine purpose for giving love and compassion to others into something frightfully unhealthy.

You cannot give what you do not have, and the counterfeit version of attaining love through approval and applause is merely an illusion of fulfillment. Its power will never break chains or set anyone free. It will only prove to break people, yourself included, as it is self-driven, self-focused, and consumed with lust and pride. Only the love of Jesus heralds the ability to feed the emaciated soul with the Bread of Life and make all things new again.

God is not moved by our outward images; He looks upon our hearts and sees the depth of our need. Hollywood is full of regular, hurting, broken people just like you and me who are merely projecting an image of perfection in the hopes of being worshiped and adored. Some of them go so far as professing to be gods and goddesses themselves, but this depraved arrogance is yielding a harvest of profound emptiness.

It's no secret that Hollywood is synonymous with words like *fake* or *counterfeit*, yet people continue to be lured by the lie that identity and value are substantiated in outward beauty and influential power. It's a very hypocritical world that screams "Be yourself and don't conform to anyone's expectations!" but then dictates the image they want you to buy into on every form of media and magazine cover.

I happen to be a leisurely collector of indigenous rocks and stones that I find in my travels around the world, and I'm fascinated by how one tiny stone can capture the essence of a mountain. I perceive human beings like these tiny pieces of majestic peaks, having been created in the image of Almighty God. We are a chip off the old block, so to speak. As a designer, my favorite are agate stones. Their rough exterior doesn't look like anything special, but when split wide-open, the contents are breathtaking and each one is uniquely different!

I believe this is an example of how God sees our beauty from the inside out. Externally we hope to reflect His countenance, but internally we are either lackluster or majestic with His energetic beauty and glory. He understands your heart's desires because He placed them there, but you will never achieve greatness by the works of your flesh. True greatness can only be built in partnership with Jesus. He develops your character as you surrender to Him and His process at work within you. There is nothing more beautiful than the prism of God's glory as His light shines from within you.

I love bold personalities, but at one time they intimidated me. Being bold is not always the same as being loud. Some of the loudest people I know are weak and insecure; I've also seen quiet people with an unwavering ability to stand alone against the crowd with their head held high.

You may not feel very courageous yet, but when God's boldness rises up inside of you, you will have a backbone of steel and nothing will be able to move you away from what you *know*. Boldness and confidence are Godlike qualities that influence others, but when they are mimicked in the flesh, they are not authentically expressed.

Dr. Michael Kerr, a family psychiatrist and Emeritus Director of the Bowen Center for the Study of the Family, points to the often difficult journey of differentiating one's self, stating, "The less developed a person's self, the more impact others have on his functioning and the more he tries to control, actively or passively, the functioning of others."[5] In my former struggle to conquer shame and powerlessness, I operated more covertly as a codependent enabler to the imperious and abusive personalities around me. It was my unhealthy belief that I somehow benefited indirectly from what I perceived as confidence from my domineering partners. But my ambiguous effort to share in their power actually caused me to relinquish control to them, which robbed me of the ability to use my true authority. In other words, they embodied certain traits that I felt I needed to embody until I came to a crossroads and recognized that my codependency was rooted in idolatry.

If you value a person or a position more highly than God, you have created an idol. It's often hardest for the sweet-natured, undemonstrative person to recognize their own idolatry or achieve accountability with God because their idol may not appear to pose a threat to anyone, or their reality may be distorted by means of control and manipulation. It took years for me to understand this, but through experienced counsel and my personal relationship with Christ, my mind and my values have been renewed.

I no longer live in the identity of shame, because I understand the enemy's assignment was to destroy me as one of God's weapons against his kingdom of darkness. My name, Brenda, in Hebrew actually means sword for the glory of God! When the enemy thought he had me, God used the raging fires to forge and prepare me for battle. We must heed the instinct to refuse whatever wants to replace the Holy Spirit in any area of our life or identity so that we can become what we were born to be.

Generational Curses

So much of who you are has been shaped by your family system. My own perceptions of reality were influenced by my familial code of beliefs and structure of corporate identity passed down through generations in my family. I am eternally grateful for the good and beautiful things that both my parents invested in my life and give honor to my father's brave efforts to rise above his own abusive family system for a good portion of his life, as well as the integrity of my mother, who strove for greater freedom in Christ than what she was taught. However, I have to acknowledge how both their unhealed wounds reinforced my own sense of victimization and how I learned to process my experiences through this filter, rather than by learning valuable lessons through consequences in my developmental years.

We are all born into a slew of influencing forces, and some of them are potentially negative. The book of Isaiah, chapter 65, makes reference to how God waits on obstinate people who walk in ways that are not good while they pursue their own imaginations. They offer sacrifices from their man-made altars (or places built by the flesh rather than spirit) and participate in things that defile them. It goes on to say that they will be paid back in full for their sins as well as the sins of their ancestors. I will refer to this as bloodline iniquities where the sins of our fathers and their fathers affect us through generational curses that must be broken by our repentance or heart change. God is never changing, and His plan is to bless us, not curse us. But we often step outside the realm of His full blessing through the things we choose to align ourselves with, often defiling our hearts, thoughts, and attitudes. These choices will bear fruit for generations, acting like curses that can only be broken when we turn our hearts to seek God as we tear down the idols that drive us to ruin.

My own father had been a victim of his parents' alcoholism and multiple forms of abuse. Instead of being advanced through the verbal blessing of positive affirming words from his mother and father, he suffered deep neglect and terrible abuse to his mind, body, and spirit by their words and deeds. This narrative, which falsely shaped his own identity, haunted him throughout his life because he didn't have a proper revelation about who or whose he really was. I truly believe the system of idolatry and wrong value system in my father's family is what drove and reinforced their abuse.

Your own family system has fashioned your governing mindsets in one way or another, and those mindsets will either equip you with wisdom and truth or cause you to lean toward negative behaviors. These mindsets are the access points for the enemy of your soul to wreak havoc on everything precious and sacred within your personhood. We are affected for generations by bloodline iniquities unless we break them through the blood of Jesus.

The word for iniquity in Hebrew is *avon*, which according to *Strong's Hebrew Dictionary* means perversity, which is evil. The idea includes fault, iniquity, mischief, sin. It comes from the word *avah*, meaning to make crooked, perverse, trouble, do wickedly wrong, commit iniquity. In its intensive form, the word is *avvah*, which means to overthrow or overturn. This type of iniquity will cause a bend or twist similar to a tree growing in the wind and, in some cases, destroying it completely. When God began to change my bent and twisted mindsets, it felt as if I had been uprooted and replanted, and I wondered if I would survive this process of inner healing. Perhaps this is what Jesus was referring to when He said He "did not come to bring peace, but a sword" (Matthew 10:34). He wants to sever the lies and unhealthy ties that have held you and other generations in bondage, and He wants to teach you that He is the door to finding restored identity.

The Bowen Theory suggests:

> A key implication of the multigenerational concept is that the roots of the most severe human problems as well as of the highest levels of human adaptation are generations deep. The multigenerational transmission process not only programs

the levels of "self" people develop, but it also programs how people interact with others.[6]

Deceptive belief systems have affected thousands of generations and caused major breakdowns in the present-day family unit. The effects of these generational wounds are continually reshaping the framework of our culture, and without God we have become a fatherless generation in need of an awakening!

In his book *The Orphan Syndrome*, Dr. Nick Eno says, "The signal trait of an orphan syndrome is the inability to find rest. There is no Sabbath."[7] When I look at my father's life, my heart still breaks because he never found true rest until he went to heaven. He lived with his guilt and shame all the way to his deathbed, and the real tragedy is that Jesus had already taken the burden for him, but the choice to enter that rest was up to him. Most victims, if not healed, become victimizers on some level because they don't recognize or understand how to restore what has been twisted at the root of their identity.

For several years I was blessed beyond words by the friendship of a precious lady who operated a licensed hair salon out of her home in North Texas. Most of my hair appointments centered on conversations about God's faithfulness over our families, children, and grandchildren. She knew a little about my testimony of healing from abuse and the process of trusting God's timing for complete restoration, but we mostly focused on our life at hand.

Pictures of her precious grandbabies lined her mirror. She always had a way of graciously ministering to my often tired body and soul while successfully making my hair beautiful within my appointment window. But one day I sensed that something was wrong. She was heavy-hearted but quiet as she placed foils in my hair. Her next appointment was an unusual no-show, so respectfully and carefully, I probed as she began to cry. She said her husband, whom I had met on several occasions, was struggling with a new job and had been living with depression for some time. She indicated there were some deep emotional issues, which had taken their toll on her, but she maintained a certain level of stoicism for his sake.

My heart broke for her because I too had lived with a spouse who was mentally ill, and I recognized a woman trying to be strong in a terribly difficult situation. She was the main breadwinner, standing on her feet for hours every day while maintaining a household and lending a helping hand to her adult children. She was the center of her family's world and the strength they all leaned upon. I knew instinctively that it wasn't good and told her that I would be praying. In hindsight though, I wish I had been more persuasive in getting her to open up more.

I related to her pain as silent tears streamed down her face when she hinted at wanting a divorce but avoided saying the words. This precious lady who worked so hard to glorify God in everything she did, a mama and grandmother who prayed diligently for her children, was in a hard place. But she didn't feel free to say too much about it.

I left her house that day with a heavy heart, not knowing it would be the last time I would ever see her again. Just a couple weeks later, as I was preparing for a live television interview, I received a text from a mutual friend informing me that the beautician's estranged husband had come to the house with a loaded handgun and shot her and her twin sister point-blank.

I felt like my heart stopped beating when I received the news. This was a man who had professed to know Christ. Yet in his brokenness and toxic state of mind, he refused accountability for his own actions and took revenge on her for setting a boundary against his abuse. I was wrecked for this family because they all lost something they will never be able to get back. She is in heaven today, I am certain of that. But the lives left in the wake of this tragedy will forever be fragmented. The enemy comes "only to steal and kill and destroy," plain and simple (John 10:10).

It may not be abuse that plagued your family—perhaps it was sickness that affected the lifeblood of your heritage. Families can also identify with their afflictions and pass a negative mentality down to their children. It's scary how quickly we accept ownership of our ailments and emotional or physical sufferings. Once we hear the doctor's diagnosis or even feel the symptoms, we begin to give it credence through verbal reinforcement.

Simply fill in the blank: "I don't feel well because of *my* _____." Or "Grandpa so-and-so had heart disease and it's genetic in our family." I'm certainly not denying the existence of pain and discomfort caused by an infirmity or discouraging the necessary preventative measures, and I'm not suggesting that any of these are a figment of the imagination. However, I do believe its important to maintain the mind of Christ when faced with any disease or affliction instead of identifying with it.

There is a difference between acknowledging illness as a part of your circumstance and allowing it to become a part of who you are. If you begin to identify with what brings you pain, you may feel victimized by life or by God, and that mindset will change the direction of your destiny. The type of mental paralysis that often accompanies an affliction-based identity can challenge some of the most basic health needs.

Divas and Doormats

We've all found humor in the funny caricatures portrayed in movies of kick-butt divas who take no hostages, and their sorry minions that follow them around. No one likes the idea of being someone's doormat, and while there's a certain appeal to being "large and in charge," it's misleading to assume that the pursuit of a dream can only be accomplished with a don't-get-in-my-way attitude. God wants you to be victorious in everything you do, but if you're going to be a conqueror in Christ, you must understand that your outward victories are preceded by your inward obedience and humility.

I'm not condemning strong personalities—quite the opposite! The Bible is full of them. What you really must decipher is what defines true strength within your own heart and attitude. People are emphatically seduced by power and greed because they are terrified of being powerless, but when the church becomes enamored with the systems and values that have built secular kingdoms, it is treading in dangerous water.

The fable about how to boil a live frog is the perfect example. It's premised on the fact that frogs are cold-blooded and adapt to their environments slowly. Therefore, if you were to hold one over boiling water, it would quickly get away because the abrupt and intense heat would make it uncomfortable. But the story goes that if you place one in a pot of cold water and slowly increase the heat, it allegedly will sit there until the water boils, tolerating the gradual rise in temperature (to its own demise).

As a young girl I remember riding in the car with my family one evening in Northern Nevada, where I grew up, and for some reason we had to veer from our normal route into an unfamiliar neighborhood, which I later found out was the red-light district. These were normal-looking one- and two-story houses with fences and lawns, except they all had large neon signs that collectively blinked a rainbow of colors against the indigo night sky. As giant flashing arrows pointed potential patrons to these establishments with names like Sue's Place, my sister and I sat wide-eyed in the back of our Lincoln Town Car, listening to our mother exclaim while Dad just kept a low profile in the driver's seat. We didn't talk much more about that experience, but it left a lasting impression on me for years to come.

Despite the fact that the area we drove through was an isolated representation of the more sinister side of Nevada's economy, its presence throughout the state was a catalyst that absolutely changed the culture. Otherwise known as the Silver State and "gold country," the beautiful high desert was riddled with many houses of ill repute in every county. Ironically, prostitution was not legal in the mid '70s and early '80s, but as a contestant in the Miss Nevada pageant, I learned that it was definitely tolerated. Consequently, our state became known throughout the world for its prostitution, in conjunction with the gaming industry, because of its tolerated presence there.

When we tolerate something, we give it permission to exist and eventually define us. If we want to prevail against the enemy, we must stop flirting with evil or looking the other way and denying any involvement. One definition of *tolerate* is "To allow the existence, presence, practice, or act of without prohibition or hindrance; permit. To endure without repugnance; put up with."[8]

The story of Jezebel in the books of Kings gives a marvelous account of how displeased God is when abusive power pulls His people away from covenant with Him and into idolatry. Queen Jezebel was the daughter of Ethbaal, a Phoenician king and priest of Baal worship. She married a king named Ahab who was considered to be the worst offender of evil in the eyes of God compared to any other king because he wanted to replace Jehovah with idolatry.

Together they erected a temple altar for Baal worship, raising false idols among God's people. Jezebel killed all but 150 of God's prophets and then became outraged at the prophet Elijah after his powerful display of God's authority at Mount Carmel, which destroyed 850 of her prophets. She was known for promoting impurity among God's people, defiling them inwardly and outwardly through idol worship and sexual immorality.

Interestingly, King Ahab conquered more land than any other Jewish king other than Solomon, yet he could not conquer the vineyard next to his palace, which was stewarded by his neighbor, Naboth. As the story unfolds, Ahab pouted and cried to Jezebel who then signed a decree in the king's name to manipulate the circumstances and have Naboth killed. It was a concerted effort to seize the inheritance, which represented Israel's promised covenant with God and the very thing Ahab and Jezebel wanted to conquer and destroy.

This same demonic scheming still exists today in the organized groups that have risen up to eradicate God's definition of gender identity and the sacredness of our sexuality as God created it. They are intent on removing the God of the Bible from our society and His laws from the laws of our land. They target the innocence of our children with an agenda to dominate the next generation and threaten our ability to witness or worship. Pay close attention, as even our language is being changed to make it more culturally acceptable and politically correct. This is a strategy intended to intimidate, control, and mute the prophetic voice of the church.

This same agenda has targeted and labeled Christians as a hate group against rampant sexual perversion, and it has set out to change the paradigm of good and evil. The movements advancing this agenda have brought multiple cases before the United States Supreme Court and raised their fists defiantly to the God of the Bible. Clearly this same spirit of Jezebel is still working on all fronts to manipulate our mindsets and intimidate truth as cunningly as it did in ancient days. Its ultimate aim is to wipe out the proclamation of God's Word by replacing it with demonic idolatry and a distorted version of the truth.

The good news is that the picture of victory for the modern-day church is evident, as Queen Jezebel's life came to an abrupt and terrible end. An officer named Jehu, who had just been anointed king by Elisha's prophet, was sent to destroy the legacy and house of Ahab. In this fascinating account of God's absolute destruction of evil, Jehu calls out for anyone who is on his side. The eunuchs who served Jezebel in the high tower called out and appeared at the window where she stood. A eunuch is a man who has been castrated to guard and serve the women of a royal court. Essentially they are made "ineffectual." But those men were quite capable when Jehu told them to throw Jezebel out of the high tower.

Do you see the parallel? Just when the church appears to be powerless and ineffective, God appoints a warrior to deliver its believers and calls them into the place of His authority. When we embrace our own inability to be effective, we must find our purpose in the authority of Christ over the principalities and rulers of darkness. It is then that we are anointed to throw evil things down.

I'm not referring to flesh and blood when I speak about the call of the Holy Spirit to cast this demonic system out of our high towers, our belief systems, and governing institutions. We will only do so by loving and serving people and obeying the instructions of heaven under the authority of Christ—certainly not by succumbing to our carnal pride. This is why it's critical to know the sound of His voice and not be fooled by another.

The bride of Christ was not called to be a diva or a doormat. She is called to be a powerful vessel of truth as she carries the light of Jesus, who was no victim on the cross. He chose to lay down His own life in exchange for yours so that you might find your life in Him and the fellowship of His sufferings. This is the only place you will be empowered with the grace to love all people.

6

||||||||||||||||||||||||

No Longer a Victim

There was no specific moment where I magically shifted from thinking like a victim of abuse to becoming a champion over it. My transformation has consisted of many different steps toward change. Multiple epiphanies, wise counsel, hard choices, and desperate prayers for courage brought down the giants plaguing my mind as I traversed through uncharted territories. It was and still is a progressive work, much like Israel's journey into the Promised Land, which required the progressive expulsion of their enemies.

I don't believe there is any such thing as an instant deliverance from the mindsets that result from a victim identity, and I would be painting a false picture of hope for you by saying there is. Our salvation in Christ is instant, but the transformation of our inward person is like the process the Israelites went through to remove all traces of Egyptian culture from their mindsets once they had been delivered out of slavery. When we accept Jesus as our Savior, we come under the protective authority of His blood that was shed to purchase our freedom from our captor, the devil. However, deliverance from the beliefs and values that once influenced our thoughts and dictated our trajectory will be transformed on the journey toward purpose. It is our willingness to follow and properly align with God's heart that will determine how long it takes for us to take hold of all that He has promised.

I had many tough situations that challenged me to adopt new perspectives after my departure from domestic abuse. I didn't have to face these challenges alone; God was merciful as He held out His hand and said, "Let's face it together." What I learned is that I no longer needed to feel threatened by someone else's bondage, which freed me from my knee-jerk responses. In this chapter we will walk through the key steps that helped me transform from victim to overcomer.

Recognize Abuse and Codependency

In the midst of my codependent enslavement, I needed an awakening to see the abuse for what it was and acknowledge that it must change. It was as if an alarm clock went off in my heart and soul, saying, "Enough is enough!" After the terrifying encounter I shared in chapter 2 when my toddler-aged daughter was in the backseat of the car during a horrific episode of abuse, I was wide awake. I realized my daughter's need for love, security, and the preservation of her innocence from both her parents, and I recognized my own responsibility to finally remove her from harm's way when it became clear that her father was not going to provide that kind of healthy love any time soon.

When God awakens you to this degree, He will also equip you with a divine exit strategy if necessary. Trust me when I say that He will make a way where there seems to be no way, and He will send you the ministering angels you need in your time of trouble if you will commit your ways to trusting Him. If you are presently in a dangerous and abusive situation, I encourage you to find an experienced counselor or safe mentor to help you face the decisions you may have to make. If your life is being threatened, you need to find a safe harbor before you can even begin to heal the assaults upon your body, mind, and soul.

On the surface you may understand the inappropriateness of these abusive acts, but your internal voice, which may have excused or tolerated the wrongs committed against you, must be reprogrammed with truth. Traditionally there has been much confusion, especially in religious circles, about setting boundaries with abuse. While that is heartbreaking to me, I am thankful that this pattern is now changing, because the church is truly a place to help heal those who have been broken by abuse. Many local ministries are now focusing on restoring victims of abuse.

At times the process of awakening and fighting the good fight can feel like hacking your way through heavy thickets and brambles. You can choose to run, or you can face it with prayer and educated counsel to find your way out of the madness. Be encouraged; you will find your way out!

My counsel came through an array of people that God assigned in my life: licensed professionals, authors, friends who became mentors, and ministers through Christian media. I will always be grateful for these amazing people who not only saw my need but also saw my potential. They invested their time, love, and prayers into me. Trust me when I say that God honors your humbled and obedient heart, and He honors your courage to face your desperate situation in partnership with Him. He will cover you and send you what you need, and you will win because Jesus has already won the battle for you.

I vividly remember feeling reduced to a puddle of tears in the solitude of my cocoon season, just after my second divorce, when one day God spoke to me directly through a verse about Israel in the book of Ezekiel. "I passed by and saw you kicking about in your blood, and as you lay there in your blood I said to you, 'Live!' " (Ezekiel 16:6). Precious friend, don't get stuck on what you look like right now or how hopeless it all may seem. God sees your *end* from the beginning, and He is faithful to finish what He has started in you. There is a jewel inside of you that He is going to bring forth into His glorious light if you'll trust the process and lean into it.

In the section in chapter 5 about generational curses, I mentioned how Jesus said He "did not come to bring peace, but a sword" (Matthew 10:34). We often crave peace when we have lived with anguish, but peace first requires healing, and this kind of healing requires surgery to remove the hindering forces in our lives in the areas we may have developed blind spots. In what areas of your life have you craved peace? Where was it absent for you in your family of origin? Who in your life might have modeled a lack of peace that triggered that same experience in you?

My lack of peace was rooted in the codependent system of enablement and control between both my mother and father. I can now recognize and recall how their internal unrest manifested in completely different areas of their lives and identities. Between my familiarity with their lack of peace and the shame that I carried from my sexual abuse, I was sabotaged in the area of healthy relational dynamics at a critical age. Dr. Murray Bowen's family systems theory that Dr. Kerr writes about views the family as "an emotional unit and uses systems thinking to describe the complex interactions in the unit. Families so profoundly affect their members' thoughts, feelings, and actions that it often seems as if people are living under the same 'emotional skin.' This connectedness makes family members interdependent."[9] Can you see how difficult the process can potentially be when Jesus begins to separate and untangle you from some of the mindsets that may have sabotaged you and generations before without your knowledge? This can happen to good people who simply lack an understanding of the issues at play.

The sword of His Word alive in us separates us from the governing forces that don't belong anymore and helps us better understand truth from a place of mercy and grace. Yes, the process of correction can be confusing and painful, but it is ultimately empowering. When you choose to lay down your old tools for new ones, you'll find the new ones to be much more effective, providing new and efficient ways to communicate, pray, and relate to others.

Before the Lord did this surgery in my own heart, I used to give love to get love, not realizing that I did not know how to love others outside of my need. This process brought me to a healthier place of relating to others and a place of authentic reciprocal love. God knows your propensity to stay in a bad situation for too long simply because you desire to be loved, but He loves you too much to let you remain in the bad habits and beliefs that will keep you there.

Religious performance was a strong motivation for me in the past. I remained in my toxic and abusive relationships because I wanted to keep my reputation clean by tenaciously doing what looked right to others, but in the process of this performance, I went even further into bondage. It may feel as if chaos will reign forever when God begins to set the crooked paths straight for you, but be encouraged that whatever part of your reputation suffers in the process of surrender and obedience, God will also restore. He is your vindicator.

See the Truth and Align with It

As I shared in the previous chapter, my foundational problem was finding identity in the wrong sources. I have learned that the enemy often contrives a counterfeit offer before we understand what our genuine purpose is. From the surface, it may even closely resemble what God has planned for you, but if just a one-degree margin of falsehood exists, it is not the real thing. The potential for gross misinterpretation of God's plan is eminent when selfish human agendas and the devil's lies are at the heart of it.

Even Jesus was tested when satan offered Him all the riches and recognition of this world. Satan even preyed upon His hunger as He fasted, tempting Jesus to choose His flesh by turning stones into bread. He then took Jesus to a high cornerstone in an attempt to make Him prove Himself as the Son of God by jumping off. Jesus was tested in His vision of the kingdom that was to come, He was tested in His flesh when it was weak, He was tested in His very identity, and as to whether He would allow pride to dictate His stance on who He was. We all are tested in these same areas today, and I wonder how it must grieve the heart of God when we dismiss the grace, peace, and humility of Jesus that equips us to overcome the temptation to perform or prove ourselves by ourselves.

The devil's deception is always meant to trick us into aligning with a counterfeit identity that feeds our lust to be noticed and our pride for achievement instead of being established in the pattern of Christ who served. I have to laugh at the picture of satan attempting to trick Jesus into bowing to him, but I also recognize his strategic timing since Jesus was weakened in His flesh from hunger and tired in His body from being alone in the wilderness where He had gone to pray.

Satan will attack you when you are at your lowest point physically and emotionally, but don't lose sight of the bigger picture. This testing took place right before Jesus' ministry began, and it was intended to abort the purpose for Jesus' birth and life. His ability to resist the enemy's lies came directly from the Father, as He aligned with heaven's will and focused His spirit on who He truly was. We must do the same to reach our own intended purpose. Remember that what you fight for today will prove to serve others in your future.

When you receive a divine revelation from Jesus Himself about who you are, you will enter a place of deep peace and marvel at the strength you have to dispel the enemy's lies without needing to prove yourself to anyone. Jesus used the Word against the enemy's lies, and we are to do the same, as it protects us from anything or anyone that is incongruous with the truth.

I have met so many women who loved Jesus from an impulsive or emotional place, but they lacked maturity and the wisdom that comes from a real relationship with Him. Sadly, these women are typically weak when it comes to the attention of men who don't have honorable intentions toward them. It's important for women to understand that there are often men who pose as believers, having a form of godliness but denying His power as described in 2 Timothy 3:1–7. The Bible talks about these kinds of people who worm their way into the homes of *weak-minded* women to take advantage of them. Such people can be male or female, and it's important to discern that they are not sent to you by God. If you want to be ready for the real relationship that God has ordained for you, gain the insight, wisdom, and discernment of Christ to send the false ones packing!

I believe this is exactly where the woman from Sychar in Samaria was when Jesus met her at Jacob's well. She had come to fetch water during the hottest time of the day from the well where Jesus was resting from His journey. When He asked her for water, He also opened the conversation to reveal her own spiritual thirst, saying, "If you knew the gift of God, and who it is that asks you for a drink, you would have asked him and he would have given you living water. … Whoever drinks the water I give them will never thirst" (John 4:10, 14). He told her to go call her husband because He knew that she did not have the true love and protection of a husband.

When she answered that she had none, Jesus said, "You are right when you say you have no husband. The fact is, you have had five husbands, and the man you now have is not your husband" (John 4:17–18). Astounded, she called Him a prophet but she was puzzled by the contradictions of her religious teaching. As a Samaritan, she asked Him why He would speak to her and why He would encourage her to worship from a different place than her ancestors did on that same mountain.

I think it's profound that He met her at the place of her worship, in the tradition of generations before her, to disrupt her religious complacency with the revelation that her true salvation would come from the sacrifice of His own blood and that the hour was coming when true worshipers would worship the Father only in Spirit and truth.

Like me, maybe you can see your own story in this account of the desperate woman at the well. I too needed to distinguish the difference between who I was and who I was pretending to be so that I could align with the truth of my Messiah. Jesus calls us to honesty about ourselves, but He also calls us to truth in our worship. This eye-opening shift is what empowered me to desire a life of obedience to the Holy Spirit where nothing is hidden from Him.

Jesus said, "I am the way and the truth and the life. No one comes to the Father except through me" (John 14:6). Once you have discovered the truth about yourself in the intimacy of His fellowship, you will identify with what He speaks to you and see yourself as He sees you. It is here that your heart will grow confident that He is your source for everything that you need. If you are stuck in the rut of attending church or listening to Bible teachers but do not feel satisfaction for your thirsty soul, I encourage you to look for the unexpected visit from Jesus on these grounds and ask Him to reveal the truth about yourself that will set you free to be fulfilled.

Forgive Those Who Spitefully Use You

Like most of us, I was taught as a child to forgive people and show kindness to everyone, but as an adult, my perception of forgiveness wavered like a pendulum wildly swinging back and forth. Quite often I was too quick to rush the process of forgiveness, accepting a disingenuous apology from someone who wasn't really repentant for what they had done.

I still remember brushing off uncomfortable dialogue, which is usually necessary for healing between two people but not always possible. On the other hand, there were those that I struggled to forgive because I felt they had betrayed or judged me in my most vulnerable situations, which poisoned me for far too long. There was evidence of two extreme reactions to offense that manifested through my root of rejection and lack of confidence, but neither of them provided a healthy solution for forgiveness.

As you begin to understand who you are in Christ, you also realize who your real enemy is. This enables you to move into the protection and authority that Jesus has given you. Incredibly, this understanding also helps you segue to the act of forgiveness, which is the gateway to your inner healing. It is so easy to view your abuser as your enemy, but there is a bigger picture that you must understand in order to break the cycle of offense and its power over you. The Bible tells us that our fight is "not against flesh and blood, but against the rulers, against the authorities, against the powers of this dark world and against the spiritual forces of evil in the heavenly realms" (Ephesians 6:12).

It is true that when you don't forgive others you only hurt yourself. Dr. Caroline Leaf so appropriately says, "Forgiveness starts with repentance, which unmasks older pathways in the nerve circuits of the brain and then as you forgive, reorganizes by rebuilding new memories over the old."[10] Wow—here is a cognitive neuroscientist with a PhD in Communication Pathology describing how God made our bodies and our brains to heal when we let go of toxic thoughts and simply choose to forgive!

The very act of repentance is to be regretful enough to change our patterns of wrongdoing and go the opposite way. That is what I finally decided to do after a lifelong habit of bearing grudges against those who had hurt me. I had to deal with the real issues, which were buried deep in my psyche, and repent of them because I wanted to be healthy and whole more than I wanted to be right.

I asked God to forgive me for carrying the unnecessary baggage of unforgiveness, as if it was something I needed to hold on to. I left those bags at the threshold of His throne of peace. Understanding that I have been given the mind of Christ and I can have compassion on the ignorance or brokenness of others instead of being hurt by them has set me free to love with no strings attached. It's also made forgiving easier to do because I understand its power.

The biggest trap for those struggling with unforgiveness is the need for control. We all want justice when we have been wronged or someone we love has been wronged, and it's all too easy to step into the role that God Himself said belonged to Him alone. He is the judge, He is the vindicator, and vengeance belongs to Him, not to us.

My husband, Paul, and I both have walked through some major tests with forgiveness, and we understand the heartbreak of betrayal. But I can assure you that when you turn control over to God and rely on Him for justice, He will not only heal your wounds, but He will also align you for His ultimate purpose. Nothing can stop or hinder His perfect will for your life other than your choice to remain in bitterness.

It's one thing to be hurt and betrayed by an unbeliever who does not view you from heaven's perspective, but when that same unbelieving mindset arises in a believer or someone you love, the cut is deeper than you can possibly bear in your flesh. I want to encourage you that when it feels as if God has overlooked or forgotten the wrong that has been done against you, He has not abandoned or forsaken you. In fact, He holds you even closer as you endure the crucible meant to purify you, because He loves you and sees you as pure gold. Like Joseph in the Bible, who was betrayed by his own flesh and blood, we learn to call out to Him from our deepest pit of pain. The power of God is not discovered in the high places or positions of authority; it is embodied in the measure of grace that is bestowed upon you in the pit of helplessness.

If you are going through painful fires and feel as if you will be consumed, I want to encourage you to sing from a pure heart where no one else is listening and let bitterness lose its grip. Watch God move on your behalf just as He did with Joseph, who waited many years for God to restore and fulfill the dream that He *knew* had been divinely placed within him.

God knew the necessary process, and He finished what He had authored in Joseph's heart so that He could place him in a position that he would rule with grace, mercy, and wisdom. As it was for Joseph, there will come a sudden moment where everything shifts in your favor because you have been proven trustworthy of the call.

Identify Healthier Boundaries

My husband and I enjoy taking road trips about once a year after the holidays to decompress, reflect on the year behind us, and look ahead to the new. It's a great time of togetherness as we experience the cultures, colors, and sounds of our beautiful country. One year while driving through New Mexico, we decided to visit the Carlsbad Caverns, which had been a childhood desire of mine. After a gradual decent of the nearly 800 feet on foot, the cavern was illuminated by lights and absolutely enchanting. But some of the steeper areas were a little daunting and flanked by safety handrails that kept hikers from falling into a dangerous abyss.

The thought occurred to me that I would not feel so confident about navigating through the depths of the earth's underground without having those rails to rely on, and that's when I made the connection! Safe boundaries in life are God's design for protection and confidence. When adhered to, they actually boost our ability and assuredness to know what lane we should be in. Imagine trying to drive your car on a towering freeway overpass at rush hour without any lane lines, signals, or guardrails to guide you. How scary would that be? This same principle applies to relationships, both with people and with God. The healthiest relationship examples have established good boundaries where honor is present and love can flourish.

God has boundaries too, and when we cross them, we grieve His heart and hurt ourselves in the process. It's called sin when we do that. However, when we respect and honor the parameters of God's Word and His Will, we can then walk in all the authority of heaven and have the confidence of knowing we are aligned with Him as His glory illuminates our way through otherwise unsafe terrain.

One of the things that secretly bothered me for years was my natural inclination toward self-betrayal. My boundaries had been violated repeatedly, but I didn't know how to communicate that or establish new healthy ones. I lamented over my self-betrayal constantly but never seemed to break the cycle. I would have rather been hurt than to defend myself, and my abusers saw this as a weakness that they could manipulate and control.

This is an area where the counseling of experienced mentors and licensed professionals really helped me to recognize the practical areas of my self-sabotage. But ultimately it was the work of the Holy Spirit who placed the backbone of truth within me and balanced it with His love. I distinctly remember the day that I began to respect the power of silence instead of allowing it to trigger me into fixing a problem that I didn't need to own.

Aggressive bullies and controllers have an arrogant way of denying responsibility for their actions, blaming everyone else instead—especially the victim of their abuse. Learning to respond to these kinds of lies requires that we first stand in a place of accountability with God. When the spirit of truth penetrates our own spirit, it changes us, and we learn that His mercy and grace is a welcome substitute for our self-condemnation. By embracing this kind of raw honesty before God, we can also embrace the reality of what has tried to destroy us and examine its actual powerlessness in spirit and truth.

I truly believe that as we grow in spirit and truth, God teaches us how to honor our bodies as the temple of the Holy Spirit and our minds as the mind of Christ. Healthy boundaries are not cruel; they are necessary for keeping us on track physically, mentally/emotionally, and spiritually. These healthy boundaries, which are rooted in God's Word, will also help propel you into your individual purpose and favor because you will not be overcome by fear any longer.

I remember the day when I had to take a phone call with my daughter's birth father after fourteen years had passed between us without communication. I had just endured the traumatic breakup of my second marriage that left my daughter and me spinning in disbelief when she decided to look up her birth father's contact information. I understood her emotional need at almost sixteen years of age to know her father, so I chose to face whatever I had to face with courage. When I picked up the phone, the dynamic between us had noticeably changed, and I was thankful for the evidence of healing in me as well as the difference in his ability to broach some of the truth about our past.

When God heals you, you will have your moment to confront the spirit of abuse that used to keep you in its cage and tell it, "No more!" Stop running from your abusers and run into the arms of Jesus. He will mend you through healthy people, teachers, counselors, and His Word. He will hold you in your dark hours of question, and before long, you will be able to recognize your abuser as the weaker one and take compassion on them through the eyes of Jesus. But you will never be controlled by them again.

Put Faith into Action and Step out of the Boat

When I had to leave two very abusive situations, it took faith to gain the courage. I could not have done what I did without knowing that God would be my source and my protection as well. I am thankful for organizations that help women who are in dire straits, and we need more of them. If you don't know where to start to find help, trust Him to connect you. He answers the prayers of those who truly seek Him.

Scripture tells us that we grow from faith to faith and that we are being transformed from glory to glory, which means each time we step outside our comfort zone and trust the Lord in faith, we grow stronger and more ready for the next level of our journey with God. As we spend time in His presence and remove the veil of pretense from our own faces, we will behold His glory and be transformed by it with every encounter.

I know this to be true in my own life, even in the midst of my repeated mistakes, as I sought to know Him more. He was faithful to see me through it all and teach me life-changing lessons. As I trusted Him with everything, little by little my eyes were opened to more truth and the kind of wisdom that began to build me up. This is a process that will always be at work in me as I spend time in His presence and trust Him with an obedient heart.

During a difficult season when my church had abandoned me and my estranged husband was stalking me, I was worshiping at home and had a vision of myself stepping out of a boat and walking on the water toward Jesus. He smiled as if I were a toddler taking her first steps and then told me to turn and look at what was behind me. As I turned, I saw a large boat filled with people who were new believers in Christ. They were dressed in white that was so bright from the illumination of God's glory that it seemed to spill from their clothing over the edge of the boat and onto the water. Then one by one, they began to step out of the boat and follow in the same steps that I had taken toward Him.

I felt the Lord speaking to my heart that day about the significance of my choice to step out of my boat and follow Him. For me, that meant trusting in Jesus instead of placing my trust in the things of this world or in the people around me. I realized that the closer I got to Him, others would follow suit as they witnessed the reality that we truly can walk on water and do what seems impossible with His help.

At that point in my life, I was being stalked and threatened by my estranged husband almost on a daily basis, and I was struggling to figure out how I would survive financially without any support. I had no idea how God would restore me, and I was far from being healed emotionally, but I knew that the only place I felt whole was in His presence. I had faith that I could trust Him and that the threats being made on my life didn't stand a chance against the Name above *all* names. Nothing could touch me outside of the realm of Jesus, and that is where I remained.

When you've been hurt and devalued by a spouse, it takes time to heal on every level, and wisdom will tell you to be more discerning about the people you surround yourself with. It will take faith, not just wisdom, for you to change your social structures. This is necessary because the wrong friends will drag you back into wrong mindsets and the kind of values that will lead you away from your source of life.

The enemy will tempt you through people who want to connect with you, and you'll need to discern the motive of their flattery. Don't trade your long-term goal of total restoration for the short-term satisfaction of your immediate desires, whether they are emotional, financial, or social. Prudence will pay off in the end!

When I moved to Dallas, I was noticed by some of the socialites and successful people that spent their time running from one event to the next. These charities and social parties were full of beautiful people who wore the best clothes and dined at the best restaurants. But I sensed that without their social circles, they would otherwise be lonely.

It was tempting to chase after the brass ring of popularity at a time that I was starting over in my life. It seemed like a way to make a name for myself and network for business, but I knew my life had been set apart for a different purpose and that God wanted to do a deep work in me. I would have stopped the process of healing and restoration had I pursued the satisfaction of my immediate emotional needs, so I chose to put my faith and trust in God alone, and He became my best friend during that time period. His favor connected me to the right opportunities, which far outweighed the high cost of fair-weather friendships.

When you truly place your whole life in Jesus' hands, a new identity grows inside of you, and you are filled with unspeakable joy on so many levels that it almost doesn't make sense. God is so patient with the process of transforming us, and He reciprocates the same sweet fellowship on a daily basis if you look for Him. He will meet your needs—all of them—and when He knows you are ready, He will bring you into a relationship that is filled with strength, honor, and purpose.

Arm Yourself with Praise

I remember days where the struggle to press through my exhaustion and heaviness felt overwhelming, and I knew that these were sink or swim moments for me. I had to choose my response to what life had handed me. I had always heard and believed that praise is our greatest weapon, but I was inexperienced in engaging something that felt so insincere when I didn't *feel* much like praising. It's so easy to shout exuberant praises to God for His goodness when we are at the pinnacle of our mountaintop experiences, but it's another thing entirely to learn the power of praise as a sacrifice in the dark musty dungeon of your emotions, where panic tries to rule over your mind.

In my travels I have been blessed to experience some amazing VIP treatment on several occasions, and my giddy praise for these amazing blessings is, I'm sure, a delight to God, because I recognize His goodness to me. But I can assure you that there is no aroma that compares to a broken and contrite heart that chooses to focus on His goodness and faithfulness in the belly of sorrow. This, my friend, is your place of true breakthrough and where you grow your spiritual muscle.

It's the place where eagles soar high above the storms on rising thermals, allowing the warm air to lift them higher and higher above the winds and the storms. God intends for us to do the same as we glide upon the warmth of His spirit and supernaturally soar above the troubles of this world. This is why the Bible tells us in Isaiah 40:30–31 (AMP):

> Even youths grow weary and tired, and vigorous young men stumble badly, but those who wait for the LORD [who expect, look for, and hope in Him] will gain new strength and renew their power; they will lift up their wings [and rise up close to God] like eagles [rising toward the sun]; they will run and not become weary, they will walk and not grow tired.

I have tested this principle of praise, and I know it to be true. My battles have all been won by the praise on my lips. Every last one of them! You cannot wait, expect, look for, or hope in God without then seeing His goodness and shifting your focus from your problem to your Problem Solver. This requires intentionality and discipline over your flesh, but as you press in with praise, the noise of your flood will subside and submit to the peace of God at work in you. I promise you it's worth every bit of your effort to praise Him in the heat of your battles.

There is a victorious army arising from the valley of dry bones where once there was death and destruction. Praise is their weapon raised against the forces that thought they had destroyed them. You can choose to stay where you are and not fight. God's love for you will remain unhindered, but there is a destiny that awaits you, and if you'll fight the good fight with your weapon of praise, you will fulfill the purpose you were designed for from your conception.

7

||||||||||||||||||||||||||||

Living in the "I Am"
of Identity

During an outing at our favorite weekend campsite, my husband and I invited our dear friends, Dan and Peggy, who lived nearby, to join us around the campfire one night. Our conversation quickly evolved into spiritually encouraging stories about God's goodness. Dan, a respected Hollywood producer with a heart full of compassion, shared his profound reflections on the lyrics of a favorite Christmas song that he'd also written an article about:

> One of the most powerful lyrics ever writ-
> ten comes from "O Holy Night" in the phrase,
> "Till He appeared and the soul felt its worth."
> When Jesus Christ left the glory of heaven and
> visited this soiled world, He brought unearned
> and unmerited dignity to all of mankind. Sinful
> human beings were bestowed value, demonstrated
> worth by the simple but incomprehensible fact

that our righteous Creator chose to come to our doorsteps. Jesus brought dignity by dining with the vilified tax collector, by granting mercy to the accused adulterous woman, and allowing the sinful woman to wet his feet with her tears. Without condoning or overlooking the damage caused by wrong or immoral behavior, Jesus first restores dignity to the brokenhearted—they are welcomed by God. And His goodness leads to their repentance.[11]

So much of our search for identity is based in the soul's desire to know its worth, and we really can't know the fullness of our true value until Christ appears to us and speaks to our limited understanding. One of the Lord's most powerful appearances came long before Jesus' birth, in the physical manifestation of His glory through a burning bush. He revealed Himself for one reason: to change the trajectory of one man who would, in turn, affect the lives of an entire nation!

Moses needed a radical recalibration for the identity whiplash he was suffering from. Caught between his humble Hebrew beginnings and the entitlement of his Egyptian court status, he suddenly had no sense of belonging at all. Ironically though, it was in his season of abasement that he gained the soul transformation necessary to fulfill his true purpose, which was to deliver the children of Israel out of the hands of slavery. As we take a closer look at the life of Moses, I think you will be encouraged to stay the course through your own season of questioning and wandering.

It's obvious that from his early days of infancy, when he was discovered by Pharaoh's daughter in a floating basket on the Nile, Moses was marked and preserved by the hand of God and destined for a purpose. However, his journey to that purpose was one filled with enormous challenge and tragedy. Clearly God ordered each and every step, intentionally favoring him to be placed as a royal son who would benefit from the finest education and material possessions available, but He didn't place him there to keep him there. It would only prove to be for a season.

Amazingly, his Hebrew birth mother was allowed to nurse him as a baby and teach him about his true heritage in the Hebrew faith during his formative years, and he would return to this spiritual foundation when he was old. As Moses grew in both wisdom and strength, he was privy to the pagan culture and perhaps even the secrets of the highest ranks of Egyptian government, which provided him a unique perspective as a trusted insider. It's no coincidence that God would use this upbringing to equip him with critical insights later to be used for a divine strategy.

In the overview of his life we can see God's master plan, but that couldn't have been obvious to Moses as a Hebrew boy with a juxtaposed identity and a deep passion for ending the enslavement of his own people. He must have been deeply conflicted as he watched the mistreatment and abuse of the children of Israel. As frustration grew within his soul, it finally erupted when he struck a slave driver who was beating an Israelite, killing him with an angry blow. In a moment's time everything shifted, and Moses realized his predicament as fear invaded his heart. Fearing for his own life, he went from living in a palace to suddenly standing on the threshold to nowhere.

As his true identity haunted him, he fled from the powers of Egypt and into the wilderness without a plan, without desert savvy, and without hope. He was confused, traumatized, and alone at forty years of age, which isn't the most ideal time of life to be starting over from nothing, especially after being accustomed to a royal lifestyle. I would imagine that at this point in his life, the mind-bending question of identity must have nagged deeply at his conscience. Having nothing and no one to draw affirmation from but the God of Abraham, his birth mother had prepared him for such a time as this in the secret meetings of his early upbringing.

At this particular intersection of his life-journey, where all his perceivable blessings have expired, his privilege and status now gone, Moses would have questioned his own survival. He had been uprooted and abandoned by everyone on the outskirts of the desert, but that's where

I personally feel the mercy of God is profoundly present. When devastating circumstances leave you questioning everything you have ever believed or everything you have been taught, it may seem like you are alone, but rest assured—He is there with you and He is all you need in this moment.

Have you too been faced with your what-ifs and all the I-told-you-so's that come with regret? Are you wishing you could go back and change the devastating domino effect that came from one decision? I'm certain that Moses was there too. In fact, I'm certain he was questioning the reason for his existence!

Sometimes we must be catapulted into the unknown so that we might discover the answers to our questions. Perhaps like Moses, you too were caught up in the identity of your success and the acceptance of people with whom you had nothing in common. Deep down, you knew you ultimately didn't belong with them, but you needed a sense of comradery.

I like to think of these seasons that serve a temporary purpose as scaffolding. The real problem arises when we hesitate to remove the scaffolding and cannot see the significance of the beautiful structure hidden behind it. Don't get too comfortable with the tools and risers that must come down so that you can be propelled forward uninhibited. And don't despair in this new season, even if your horizon looks bleak. You are about to encounter God's glory like you've never seen, and every God-given gift from your past will serve its own purpose as He intended.

Subsequently, what felt like a futile ending to Moses was, in actuality, a new beginning. It's seasons like these that reveal God's unending patience as they develop our own. For another forty years Moses lived in the wilderness, preserved and provided for as a stranger in a foreign land where he faithfully shepherded another man's flock of sheep. Far removed from the glory days of his past, by now it would seem logical that he'd lost every ounce of confidence in his ability to manage anything but a bleating herd.

Finally, at nearly eighty years of age and stripped of his dignity, he has a God encounter that absolutely rocks his world. Isn't it ironic that God chooses to meet us on the outskirts of our broken dreams instead of at the altars of our egos? This is the place where pride has been dethroned and we have no hope left but God. As Moses traversed the arid terrain that day, which probably felt like any other day after forty years of shepherding and serving others in a strange land, God showed up in a burning bush.

The Bible account tells us that he noticed the bush was oddly not consumed, which I'm certain turned his ordinary day into an extraordinary one. As he curiously walked toward the fiery bush, He heard God's voice coming from it and was instantly afraid for his life! I find it profoundly moving that when we are at our lowest point, God chooses to reveal His power, His grace, and His glory in a unique and personal way so that we might be built back up and transformed into His image.

Amazingly, He dignifies us when we think we are castaways. As soon as God spoke to Moses, he turned his face because he was afraid, and God told him not to come near but to take off his shoes, "for the place where you are standing is holy ground" (Exodus 3:5). This is one of the most beautiful and poignant portrayals of pure worship that I can think of. The emphasis here is on humility and vulnerability, as Moses feared the Lord because he knew he was in the presence of Almighty God.

Through Christ, we have been given the freedom to come before God's throne boldly, but if you are not undone in His presence and overcome by the absolute awesomeness of who He is, you haven't comprehended the fact that without His mercy we would all be consumed. You cannot understand the measure of His love without fathoming His greatness swooping in to meet us in our lowliness, and without this you may have encountered religion but have yet to bask in His life-changing presence. First Corinthians 1:29 tells us that no flesh will glory in His presence. Such a sobering yet joyful thought as I reflect on my personal encounters with Him. God met me in my weakest moments, and the impact of encountering His glory in the place of my shame has changed me forever.

Our human temptation is to approach God with our trophies and badges of honor to offer Him all that we believe we do best, but that's actually the opposite of what God is looking for from us. He wants our hearts. We have nothing to offer anyone while our ego is attached to our sacrifice. It's only after our store has been emptied and then refilled with greater substance than what we can accomplish on our own that God can use us powerfully.

This is where Moses was when God called him and spoke over his identity, changing it from failed wanderer to powerful deliverer. God supernaturally equipped a broken man in his old age who by now was even struggling with his ability to speak. Yet in God's eyes, Moses would be a stealth bomber, strategically commissioned to confront the demons of hell and lead his people out of slavery into a land flowing with milk and honey!

All it took was one genuine encounter with the Great I Am to change his perspective about himself and his purpose. This is where he was equipped to lead God's chosen ones to destiny. He most likely was afraid when he thought about where he'd been for the past forty years. That's usually how we start reasoning with God when He calls us at our weakest moments.

I know I have questioned Him, asking, *But, Lord, why would you call me now? My best is behind me. I'm not capable as I once was—in fact, I'm terrified to even try!* This is what keeps me dependent on God and focused on what it's all about. It is not, and will never be, about me; it is about what He can do through me—or anyone—willing to truly follow Him. The only thing left in Moses' hand at this point in his life was a wooden staff that he used to herd sheep.

What a glorious picture of choosing to obey God authentically, just as you are and nothing more, so that real miracles can happen to set real people free. God revealed to Moses what He could do through his mediocrity by turning a wooden staff into a serpent, and from that day forward, he trusted the Great I Am and obeyed Him with all that he was as he discovered his completeness in Him. God wants to pour His power and glory into whatever is in your hand, and I've witnessed this in my own life to be true.

Moses' staff may as well have been the scepter of heaven when he used it to carry out God's orders. You may think your ordinary tool or talent is too simple or small and unattractive, but I want you to know that the only thing important to God is your availability and your humble heart as you stand before Him, seasoned in love and ready to obey His call. You are not finished, my friend—you are just beginning, and He has big plans for your life!

When the enemy thinks he has stolen your past, don't let him have your future. Find your belonging and identity in the Great I Am, and you will find your destiny to change the world around you. The most assuring part of this story is that Moses would not have to go forward alone. He was clothed in the glory of heaven as God told him, "Do not fear, I will be with you," and when Moses asked what name he should refer to Him by, God answered, "I AM WHO I AM, This is what you are to say to the Israelites: 'I AM has sent me to you'" (Exodus 3:14).

My own life-collision with God also came on the back side of my wilderness, and all my preconceived notions about who He was and who I thought He wanted me to be were overridden by a brand new revelation. Like Moses, I had a false sense of who I once was long before all my trophies tarnished and turned to dust. This is the relevance of what I previously addressed regarding generational curses and the iniquities of the fathers.

It is helpful to understand that a bloodline iniquity is what causes a defect in our thinking and causes us to gravitate toward certain behaviors and mindsets like a young tree growing in the path of a constant wind. If there is no sturdy rod of truth to train it upright, it will lean in whatever direction its environment prompts. This is why I am so grateful for my mother's teaching and prayer, which became my training rod of truth.

I believe the season of obscurity on the back side of my own wilderness provided the necessary uprooting, which helped retrain my thoughts and straighten out the crooked places in my life. It was not easy to see the big picture at that time while I was caught up in the process of my own unraveling. Sometimes I felt as if there was no chance for anything good to come out of my bad choices, but God used it all to rebuild me for a greater purpose than I had ever known. When I look back on it all today, I realize the need for the process and the supernatural revelation, which broke down every thought that tried to get in the way of what God wanted me to see.

When I finally let go of the false image of myself that I'd become enamored with and took a deeper look at my pain in the mirror of God's glory, my reflection revealed not only His love for me just as I was but also my understanding of who He had planned for me to be all along. This was the well that my deepest worship came from. You might say it was my alabaster box that I was honored to break open before the feet of Jesus and pour out the contents of my life and my love like anointing oil.

Once you see yourself in the reflective light of Jesus' love, you no longer need to find your value in the temporal things of this world or the shallow versions of strength and beauty that so quickly become idols or objects of our worship. In His light, His glory will consume you—body, soul, and spirit—as it redefines your indisputable birthright and hands you the destiny that no one can take away.

The book of Genesis says we were created in the image of God, so we must first know who He is from our own interactions with Him (not just what we've been *told* about Him) in order to begin the process of knowing ourselves. We cannot truly see ourselves until we have peered into His glorious image in the fellowship of His presence.

When God told Moses that His name is "I AM," He said, "This is my name forever, the name you shall call me from generation to generation" (Exodus 3:14, 15). The same revelation of His glory is as much for us today as it was for Moses, and this is the holy ground where we discover that nothing is broken or missing.

One of the most beautiful illustrations I've heard on the subject of the Great I Am is described by Jonathan Cahn in *The Book of Mysteries*:

> God's name is made up of four Hebrew letters (the yud, the heh, the vav, and the heh—YHVH meaning I AM). The name of eternal. We say His Name when we say our own, "I am _____." It is woven into the fabric of existence that when you speak of yourself, you must first say His Name. Your existence comes from His existence. Your I am only exists because of His I Am.[12]

The most common method of identifying or attempting to affirm one's identity is to say one's name, and the meaning of a name is significant to the characteristics that define us. As a matter of fact, when God transformed the identity of people through their encounters with Him, He often changed their name as we see in both the Old and New Testaments. Jacob (the deceiver) became Israel (the chosen), and Saul (the persecutor of Christians) became Paul (the apostle). We do not have the ability on our own to affirm anything more than our defining characteristics, but God affirms and completes us. He can affirm "I AM" without saying anything else as His eternal self-existence defines Him, but our existence doesn't define us as anything more than a creature created by another, namely God.

The definition of *identity* is described as "the condition of being oneself or itself, and not another. Exact likeness in nature or qualities."[13] It's where we get the word *identical*. When we try to define our own identity without drawing it from God, who is the fullness of being, we are left to extract inspiration from creation rather than the Creator who made us and this produces an inauthentic copycat or counterfeit. However, when we place our admiration and desperation toward God, we become like Him and are empowered to be who He actually created us to be. Apart from God (YHWH—I AM) it is impossible to comprehend our likeness to His image or nature within us.

Jesus said, "If I glorify myself, my glory means nothing. My Father, whom you claim as your God, is the one who glorifies me. ... Before Abraham was born, I am!" (John 8:54, 58). Essentially, He was confronting the hypocrisy of religious pride, which can also become a form of identity to some. It's the error of relishing in any glory that comes from our performance. Jesus lived in the I Am of identity, and when He gave His own life for ours, He paved the way for us to do the same. He made it possible for us to be reunited with the Father so that we might understand who we truly are and the fullness of our identity in the light of His glory.

If you want to be authentic, you must draw from the source of origin. Jesus said, "I am the bread of life" (John 6:35), "I am the light of the world" (John 8:12), "I am the gate [to the Father]" (John 10:9), "I am the good shepherd" (John 10:11), "I am the resurrection and the life" (John 11:25), "I am the way and the truth and the life" (John 14:6), and "I am the true vine" (John 15:1). He was the Great I Am in the flesh, so if you want to be whole, filled with light, connected to the Father, guided by His Spirit, live eternally, and walk in the truth, you can only do that by knowing Jesus. And that is where you will finally know yourself. He is the "I am" of our identity and the shalom, peace, blessing, favor, and fullness of our existence. He is the horizon of hope drawing you into His open arms so that you might live in the completeness of the Great I Am.

There are many names for God in Scripture, and they make up an exhaustive reference to His infinite characteristics and who He is. However, the name "I Am" is a statement of totality that encompasses everything. Nothing is missing under the blanket of I Am. When Moses faced his ultimate purpose, he was stripped of his human glory and weakened by age, yet the full array of I Am was with him, went before him, and was his rear guard. Even though Moses was at a state of ultimate weakness, the strength, power, and glory of I Am was made manifest, and as he walked in that covering and covenant, he became enough!

Even as I write from a remote corner of a nearly vacant café, warm tears gush over my cheeks because I cannot help remembering the same power of the Great I Am infusing my own tattered life with His presence and anointing. By anyone else's standards I might be considered the least likely to write a book on identity, but it's the process of God's transforming work within me that qualifies me to give account. Like Moses, I was an imposter in a glamorous world where I'd found great favor for a season. My mother was also a woman of unwavering faith and consistent prayer as she taught me my heritage and poured every ounce of her love into the formative season of my life.

I weep when I realize the value of a praying mother. Especially the ones who have paid a high price for the kingdom of God to be first in their lives and their children's lives. My mom believed in me no matter the circumstance or how far into the pit of deception I fell because she had dedicated my life to the work of the Lord when I was conceived. Despite the string of disasters and failures that have cluttered the path behind me, I discovered the Great I Am and my own true value in His merciful embrace.

He is also the Great Shepherd, and He will leave the ninety-nine to run after the one lost sheep from His flock. At the lowest point of my life, He did the same for me, and His mercy transformed me from the inside out when I saw His unfailing love for me. Finally, I truly understand what it means to be the daughter of the Most High God. It has nothing to do with what I have produced or what anyone says about me. Nothing to do with the labels that others try to place on me. But it has everything to do with the price He paid with the gift of His Son as a ransom for my life and the reciprocal nature of our covenant relationship that allows me to walk in His divine authority and promise every single day.

As a believer in Christ, whether a new babe or a seasoned follower, you have been equipped with supernatural power tools to carry out the plan God has had for your life since the moment of your conception. And you cannot build anything of eternal value without them. He loves you so very much, and I believe that is the reason you are reading this book! Ask Him to reveal Himself to you in a way that will change the trajectory of your life. I promise you that you will begin to recognize His presence and His fingerprint on the smallest details of your life. He will speak to you in quiet moments and even in chaos to provide revelation and understanding where you long for answers. He is as close as your asking when you seek with a hungry heart. Life and identity begin at the source of life itself, and it is in Him that you will discover your unshakable identity and the truest happiness known to mankind!

8

|||||||||||||||||||||||||

The Miracle of Rebirth

After my mother passed away quite unexpectedly, my sister and I, along with our daughters, were suddenly faced with the loss of our beloved matriarch. She was the glue that held our family together and a consummate encourager playing a crucial role in the development of our faith. To lose her so suddenly felt as if our foundation had been ripped away by an unforeseen storm. Shortly after her passing, my daughter, who thought of her gram as a second mama, began seeing butterflies everywhere—even out of season. It's fairly common to notice unusual things when someone you love has gone, but this phenomenon seemed to grab her attention because it was so out of the ordinary.

After a continual pattern of beautiful sightings and incidents of large butterflies landing on her feet, she began to study the miracle of their metamorphosis. Suddenly, what seemed like coincidentally odd occurrences began to feel divinely ordained. God knows our need, and He has great compassion for the brokenhearted. Perhaps He was sending her a message of the miracle in a butterfly's rebirth. Perhaps I too needed to be reminded of the beauty that comes out of such tremendous pain. Once again, God spoke to me in my place of deep loss.

Once a caterpillar has gone through its full life cycle of leaf gorging, rapid growth, and continual molting, it is ready for a copious encounter with something magnificently different than it has ever known. Inside the genetic blueprint of its DNA is a new body plan, which begins to form inside of something called a chrysalis or butterfly pupa. But transformation comes at a price for the caterpillar. It must lose its life in order to find it.

During this quiet pupal stage, every part of a caterpillar, from its exoskeleton to its nervous system, is liquefied to provide the necessary sustenance for its soon-to-be adult life. One might think there is nothing left but death inside of this tiny little tomb where its occupant no longer identifies as a caterpillar but is still not yet a butterfly. It has been utterly demolished for the sole purpose of rebuilding and becoming what it was always intended to be. How I marvel at the hand of God, who carefully watches over this secret thing of beauty in the making.

While the pupa is filled with the decomposed remains of what once was, tiny cells called imaginal discs start to bring new body parts into being. Isn't this just like God? When we feel we have been pulverized into nothing but decomposed matter and are alone and afraid of what we cannot yet see or understand, He speaks to our imagination and gives us glimpses of what is to come! Jesus prophesies life to come forth from our death before we are ever able to envision it.

Once reformed, the butterfly reveals its own unique colors, patterns, and wing shape, and it prepares to emerge from its restrictive space. As it inflates and expands its body, the pupal exoskeleton splits and a new creature emerges. This is an especially critical part of the process for the butterfly to be able to take flight, because as it struggles out of the cocoon, blood is pumped into its wing veins to keep them flexible as they unfurl to take flight for the first time.

Without this necessary struggle, these wings that were formed so intricately and beautifully would remain hardened, and the butterfly would die never having taken its intended flight. I cannot help but compare this manner of hardening to the often terrible effects of emotional wounding, which can potentially cement people to bitterness and cause them to stop believing in a faithful God. New life requires forgiveness, not only of past abusers but also of those who are incapable of offering a helping hand or even a word of encouragement in your rebirth process. Only then can you embrace the childlike faith that will catapult you into greater purpose.

There have been several seasons of rebirth for me where I have had to bear down and intentionally fight forward. To be honest, each time I wasn't sure that I could make it to the finish line. Being an encourager by nature, I needed the encouragement of others. But instead I felt overlooked, misunderstood, and even judged for not being what people expected of me. I knew it was up to me and no one else to believe and trust the power of Christ residing within me as my strength to overcome. Such was the case both times I had to leave an abusive marriage, losing many of my friends and church supporters in the process. But I found Jesus to be more real than ever in each and every scenario. My most recent struggle involved losing the biggest encourager of my life—the one person I could always consistently count on.

Looking back, it must have been by God's design that I happened to be talking with my beautiful mother on a FaceTime video call the very moment that she startlingly passed. I had just met a high-pressure deadline, and Paul had hand-delivered me a glorious array of long-stemmed red roses for our wedding anniversary. I called to share the beautiful flowers with her. I was in Florida and she was in Texas. I was expecting to hear that she was feeling better after having been ill for a couple of days. Sitting in her comfortable recliner wearing a pretty periwinkle blouse, she was still pale from the apparent toll it had taken on her body.

It was a chaotic time for every member of our family as each of us were scattered in different directions. Mom had been dealing with the unwelcome task of insurance red tape after months of living with flood damage, and the painting crew had just finished for the day. When I called that afternoon, I could hear my sister in the background, and we discussed how concerned we were for Mom, although she had been adamant about not wanting to go to the hospital. My sister decided to run to the store for electrolytes at Mom's request, just after giving her some cold watermelon in the hope that it would help stabilize her energy while I remained on the phone with her.

I informed her that I planned to fly home the very next day to help her get well, and she resolutely told me not to, saying she wanted me to keep doing what I was doing. At the time I was working on the beginning stages of a book deal and also working with my husband in the media field. She seemed to be somewhat soothed by the chill of watermelon when she began to describe what had felt like waves coming over her for a few days. Something felt off, but I couldn't put my finger on it. As I started to search for flights home, she said something and suddenly looked me in the eyes as if to both give and receive comfort.

She grabbed her forehead with one hand saying, "A wave!" I asked, "Mama, are you okay? Are you nauseated?" My mind raced like a wild horse trapped in a starting stall as I tried to assess what might be wrong. I was 1,200 miles away and feeling pretty helpless on the other end of the phone. Only seconds had passed before she dropped her phone in her lap, and all I could see was her pretty periwinkle blouse. Hearing only noises and seeing no movement, I screamed over and over again, "Mom! Mama! Mom, pick up the phone ... Please, pick up the phone!"

She was unresponsive, and I had to force myself to hang up with trembling hands so that I could call my sister for help. Still ten minutes away, she bravely raced back home only to find Mom slumped over and the half-eaten bowl of watermelon spilled on the floor. Through hyperventilating cries, I heard her scream as I answered my phone, "Sis, she's gone, she's gone!" The paramedics immediately rushed through the door, pushing my sister aside to begin their work on Mom. I went numb as I heard her plead with them to save our mom. After they ordered my sister to step outside, together we called on the authority of heaven, speaking life into our mother's lifeless body and pleading with God for a miracle. We wept together in the spirit for over ten minutes until we quietly and soundly resolved our trust in Him.

Something peaceful swept over my spirit as our prayers came to a close, and I heard myself say, "Sis, there will only be one reason if she does not come back to us—because she would rather be home with Jesus. She loves Him more than anyone or anything, and she's waited her whole life to see Him face-to-face!" She agreed and the paramedics wheeled the gurney out through the front door of my mother's home, stating that they had a very weak heartbeat.

As I clung to the phone, longing to take my mother's hand and kiss her sweet face, my sister called out, "Mama, we are here and we love you—we are praying!" My heart broke for my baby sister in the wake of such trauma, for my daughter who was frantically fighting Dallas traffic and crying unquenchable tears to get to her gram, and for our sweet Poppie, who had married our mama twelve years prior. He loved her like a princess and became a father figure to us all. Mom didn't make it to the ER; her heart stopped beating enroute to the hospital where my family was given the very hard news. I received the dreaded phone call while in a grocery store parking lot and wept alone in my car.

Suddenly a lifetime of memories, our love for each other, and Jesus were all my family and I had to hang on to. We were a company of survivors with broken hearts, having to figure out who we were without the one person who had encouraged us all to never give up on God. Most of the condolences and compassionate prayers that came were from people who didn't know my mother or the significance of her voice in my life after years of abuse. I feared giving the impression that I was an immature mama's girl and did my best to embrace this new season without her, despite my regret that she was much too young to die.

I knew God was calling me to a higher place where I would yet discover a stronger, more graceful me in the process of acknowledging my grief and finding my peace. Losing my mother has forced me to dig deeper than I would have otherwise with her here. It has taken me where there are no words for prayers, just a groaning of the Spirit in the Holy of Holies, and it has forced me to face and accept the cold hard truths of my past as I dared to open Pandora's box again. Grace is what pushed me through when I wanted to give up. The timing of this book is not lost on me, nor is the infinite wisdom of God's ways, which are higher than my own.

In every level of rebirth, I have had to overcome the temptation to be offended at others, especially those who had the power to help me during my struggle. I realize now that many of them understood that the difficult process was intended for me alone to conquer, but some were simply judgmental and lacked compassion. In the heat of battle at times, it can feel as if no one cares about what you've been through or understands the level of opposition you have encountered. I can assure you though, that in your obedience to follow the call of God on your life, this is part of what will release you from the opinions of people. When we think we need help from others, only God gives us sufficient grace to endure the fight!

This is the place where you realize you must quit complaining and focus your energy on getting out of the place you are in. You will see this begin to bear fruit in every area of your life as it applies to your relationships, your health, your finances, and anything else you steward over. Understand that God has equipped you, and it is His voice calling you forth in this transition. You were not destined to struggle forever, and you must be calculated about where your fight is as you partner and align with Almighty God! If during birth a baby stays in transition for too long, it will be harmed. The transition and the struggle are always for a greater purpose. Just keep going—new life is on the other side.

What I pray you perceive is how critical your fight is when you are struggling to come out of your cocoon. You may feel abandoned in the process and wonder why you're here, but it's very important that you keep your heart and mind submitted to the Lord and that you rejoice as the process unfolds. You must fight through your weariness, fight through your panic, and fight through the voices that tell you to give up! You are literally in your birthing room, and every woman who has given birth knows that this is not a pretty sight. Similar to the process of giving birth to a new baby, your rebirth involves spectators who offer very little help and sometimes criticism. You are vulnerable in this place as the process pushes you to the brink of your tolerance, and you'd do almost anything to not have to finish, but you know you cannot go back—the only way out is forward.

Without intentionally deciding to engage your faith in fight mode, the soft and tender places of your heart might be easily offended, causing it to crystallize before you ever realize the gift that awaits you on the other side of your struggle. This pain will produce such beauty, and you will not suffocate in the process because He is with you and He makes a way where there seems to be no way at all. In previous chapters, I shared about some of my daughter's challenging tests, each of which felt so undeserved because she had gone through so much at such a young age. What might your tests have been and how have they affected you? The story of the butterfly is one that we can all identify with, and I'm so thankful that God not only changes us in the chrysalis but also watches over and preserves us as we struggle to emerge as a new creature.

Maybe you feel like the caterpillar worm right now, filled with insecurity and overwhelming shame that makes your skin crawl, but you're oh so hungry for more than where you are. God doesn't see you as a worm—He sees you as whole and beautiful through the blood of His Son. He is continuously in the process of finishing the work that He began within you, to redefine your understanding of who He is and who you are in Him. He has placed something so beautiful within your spiritual DNA that you will not be able to see until it has come through the process of rebirth in Christ. I want to gently encourage you to eradicate the lie of shame as you examine yourself in the mirror of God's Word if a shame-based identity has kept you from seeing your own potential. He sees your end from the very beginning, and He will rescue you from all that tried to stop you from becoming everything He designed you to be. It is never too late to find the new you that He waits so patiently to give.

Perhaps you have been pulverized by unwelcome tragedies and disappointments in your life that have not led you to your dreams but to the back side of loneliness instead. You, dear friend, are in your cocoon.

Embrace the process and invite Him into your pain, your longing, and your loneliness. Trust His timing because He has not forsaken you. By His divine order, I assure you that He will turn your sorrow into dancing and make you brand-new again. You may have lived your life serving Him the best way you knew how to, but you are being recalibrated for a better way in this season, just like the old wineskins Jesus talked about in Matthew 9:17. They had to be conditioned and immersed in water and oil before they could receive new wine. He has saved the best for last, my friend, and you are about to receive the fullness of His loving promise if you simply remain in Him and *believe* in the developmental process.

Don't let the enemy harden your heart or distract you from where God wants to take you. Fight for your life by immersing yourself in the Spirit of God when nothing else makes sense. There have been countless times that I have taken my wounds and offenses to God and worked them out with Him. Nothing can bring you the peace and courage you need if you allow disappointments to take your fight and channel it toward the wrong things. You are going to need every bit of your strength and focus to make it to the next level, and you will get there through the grace and peace of Jesus. In my heart of hearts, I want to urge you to let Him fill you with faith and purpose for the journey, knowing that He has much loftier plans and purposes for you than allowing you to remain a stagnant caterpillar who simply eats, molts, and crawls. You will never become what God has revealed to your spirit as long as you carnally relate or operate from this ground level. As you overcome, you will be a reflection of His glory and take flight with the unique markings and colors that represent exactly who you are in Christ. No one will ever have the power to take that away from you.

There is purpose in your pain, beloved, and God, in His Word, has promised, "I have chosen and not rejected you. Do not fear, for I am with you; do not be dismayed, for I am your God. I will strengthen you; I will surely help you; I will uphold you with My right hand of righteousness" (Isaiah 41:9–10 BSB). I can still remember the physical and emotional exhaustion I felt when I had to press through the struggle of overcoming my limitations. I had outgrown the stage of life I was in, and yet I wasn't quite ready for what I believed and longed for in my spirit. This is definitely a place of pressing, but with God, you will come out a winner.

He has placed His own fingerprint on the DNA of your future, and you are coming out different than you were when you entered your last season. You are unique and loved more than you could ever imagine. Embrace your brilliant colors as you see your wings unfold. They will be the very thing that will attract others to the life of Christ within you and draw them to know Jesus the way you have while in your chrysalis. Greater is He that is within you than he that is within the world.

Now that I am no longer chained to the limited thinking that I used to live by, I am flying on my own, and from this vantage point I am able to see others as Jesus sees them without feeling threatened or afraid of their human condition. I embrace the priceless value of people as they are to God, the Father, and I also can often see their pain. I recognize the journey as one that I used to travel, and I have deep compassion for those who have no hope. "The Spirit of the Lord is on me, because he has anointed me to proclaim the good news to the poor. He has sent me to proclaim freedom for the prisoners and recovery of sight for the blind, to set the oppressed free, to proclaim the year of the Lord's favor" (Luke 4:18–19).

We all are called to speak life where it may not exist, as though it already does. Once you have experienced the transition of coming from darkness into light, you will be able to call to the life that wants to be in someone else, just as Jesus did for those who needed to see a vision of new life through His eyes. Your vantage point changes when you have found your new identity in Christ and the power to take flight, because you're no longer limited to crawling in the low places where emotions rule and dictate your fate.

Jesus spoke life to everyone He encountered. He gives us hope for a future when no other person knows how to love or accept us. He called for Lazarus to come forth when he had been decomposing in a tomb for days, giving us an example of His power to raise the dead. One of His most poignant examples of speaking life was when He called Simon Peter "the rock" (Matthew 16:18). Jesus had the foresight to discern Peter's weakness that would cause him to deny Him three times, yet He called him the rock that His kingdom would be built upon. He was speaking to the person Peter would become in Christ and not to his flesh.

In the book of Matthew, Jesus and the disciples had just finished the Last Supper and reached the Mount of Olives when Jesus informed them that on this night they would all be scattered after falling away from Him. Peter emphatically declared his loyalty to Jesus, stating that even if everyone else fell away, he never would. Jesus answered Peter, "Truly I tell you, … today—yes, tonight—before the rooster crows twice you yourself will disown me three times" (Mark 14:30). How profound that even in his most passionate intentions, Peter denied Christ before the sun came up. I believe he needed to face the truth of who he *wasn't* in his own strength, before he could become who he would be in the hope and identity of Christ.

Peter was eager to please Jesus as he passionately loved and followed Him with his whole heart, but this divine revelation introduced humility to a zealous man who had already been renamed for His purpose by Christ Himself. This experience transformed him into a man now bowed on bended knee, knowing that he too was capable of denying Christ and needed God's grace to begin again. His passion was still intact and all of his natural abilities, but his pride had taken a seat to the Son of God, in whom he now found his identity.

When Jesus truly becomes our source for existence and we've really seen how broken we are in our flesh, we recognize how much we need a Savior. This is what Jesus was referring to when He said, "Upon this rock I'll build my church" (Matthew 16:18 KJV). Peter was an unlikely candidate to lead the early church, but once transformed by grace, he was ready to become what God had intended for him through the mercy of Christ. Jesus had the foresight to comprehend that His divine revelation of identity within Peter would be the rock that the modern-day church would be built upon.

The same is true for you and me as we find ourselves in His love, acceptance, and Word of life that awakens us. Jesus sees what we cannot see with our human eyes. The DNA of your Creator lives within you and has made your spirit responsive to the call of life. As I write, I am calling to the dead thing inside of you today and telling it to live. You may think your time is up or you may be afraid to try again, but Jesus Himself prophesies to you from the entrance of the sepulcher where you have been buried in your sorrow. He sees you as brand-new, and I do too. I echo His words of affirmation over you and His perfect love as I tell you to fight forward, casting all your fears aside. You're about to enter your renewal.

If you only know Jesus as a teacher or a Bible figure and have yet to know Him as the lover of your soul and your hope of salvation, you too can know Him just as I have discovered Him. His love for me isn't any greater than His love for you, and I'm certain that you are the reason I am writing this book today. You are the reason I have chosen to fight intense battles and press through every obstacle that tried to make me give up and prevent me from sharing my story.

If I could wrap my arms around you right now and say, "Go deeper with Jesus," I would. I would cry with you just as He weeps with you over the assaults that have come against you. They were never from Him! I would celebrate the hope of new life that only He can bring and encourage you to run after Him with all you've got. There is no greater compassion that you will ever receive than the compassion of the Lord, and I know He cares for the lost and the forgotten. He has come to mend your broken heart and make it new again.

Who else but the Son of God could ever endure such a brutal crucifixion and see it through to completion. When He suffered, He was not a victim, because He chose to be there. He had you and me on His mind and love is what kept Him there. Love is what brought Him back from the grave to bestow you with the keys to life, and He stands with you now, opening His arms to receive you instantly. He chose you, and I pray that you'll now choose Him. If you want to know Jesus personally and give Him the reins to your heart, your life, and your identity, all it takes is asking Him right now. He will hear you!

You can say it like this: "Heavenly Father, I accept Jesus as your Son, and I welcome the gift of eternal life that you have given to me freely, through His sacrifice on the cross. I want to know you and to live for you. I've done things my way for long enough, but today I'm placing you in charge and committing my whole heart to you. I trust you! Thank you for loving me just as I am, and thank you for the hope of your promise to restore me to your original plan and purpose for my life. Help me walk closely with you and grow in this relationship as we journey together. Be the life-light inside of me that guides me home."

In my heart I believe you did choose Him just now, because I have been where you are and have witnessed the overwhelming, all-consuming love of God the Father, through Christ, His Son, and the Holy Spirit. He is with you right now, and you are a brand-new creature! There is no sweeter thing than to find yourself in the fullness of Him. Welcome to a love like you have never known. You are about to find your wings as you rest in the peace that you have always longed for!

9

|||||||||||||||||||||||||

The Paradox
of Selflessness

You're a new creature, and I celebrate with you and all of heaven as you embark on your life in Christ! But you might be asking yourself, *Now what?* Let me assure you that as a child of God, your steps are divinely ordered and He carefully watches over you as you take each and every one. He gives His angels charge over you to help fight for you. What an awesome thing to know that we are so loved and protected by the hand of Almighty God. Your journey will entail learning to trust Him as you build your relationship with Him through communication (prayer), dedication, and worship.

Worship is simply the gratitude of one's heart that boasts in God's glory and His goodness and greatness. It is expressed through our words, our work, our service to others, and even through music and dance. Worship is more a position of the heart than it is an action or a statement. It's always the heart and the motive behind our actions and words that determine true worship. God looks upon the heart, and that is where He sees our beauty. It is where you will feel Him molding you into a glorious portrait of His perfection and creating the beacon that your light will shine from.

It's our natural human tendency to place value on what we do or to focus on how much monetary value and status we attain, which feeds the problem of classism in every culture. Our world is full of desperate people looking for significance, and consequently, they focus on fixing the image of themselves that they believe others perceive rather than finding the answers to their longings from the ultimate Source. It doesn't matter how far you've climbed on the social ladder or how low you might think you are—to God you are priceless, and that is the truth you must set your sights on.

A new butterfly does not focus on its own beauty; it is too busy enjoying its new life and freedom after having been a ground crawler for so long. It has something to celebrate as it becomes a harmonious part of the greater symphony of nature, making sweet worship to the Creator. Just as the rocks and stars cry out to Him, how much more does a newborn butterfly? How much more should you and I? True worship cannot be conjured. It only springs forth from our fountain of love when we realize how much He has first loved us!

As a matter of fact, the dance of a butterfly is so beautiful that to encounter one as it comes near seems to lighten even the heaviest heart. That is what you and I are like to someone who has not found his or her wings yet. We are like a breath of life or a ray of sunshine to those who need hope, and we are called the salt of the earth to those who hunger for more. This is because the Spirit of the Lord is upon us, and His light shines from within us in order to draw others to Him.

It is pure deception that leads people to focus on themselves. As followers of Christ, we are gifted with a highway to victory instead of the low road that the world offers. Our examples for the better way are found in Christ Himself. We don't focus on ourselves to improve ourselves. Instead, our focus is on losing ourselves so that we might find ourselves in Christ alone. A focus on our self produces selfishness, and that is the old nature we must crucify by yielding our ways to God's ways. When we focus on Jesus, we become more like Him and discover true power and perfect peace.

God makes us new creatures, and He is the one who empowers us to follow Him. In Matthew 16:24, He instructs us: "Whoever wants to be my disciple must deny themselves and take up their cross and follow me." There is a beautiful paradox that takes place when you choose to surrender to God. I know from experience that out of the night comes the day, out of laboring pain comes abundant joy, and out of sowing comes reaping. The paradox of selflessness holds the secret to living in real freedom. Enslavement to sin, addiction, and bondage will no longer have a hold on you here because it cannot touch you when you are living in Christ alone. You are walking in a new covenant and identity now, so the power of Almighty God and all the authority of heaven dwells within you.

As a new creature in Christ, I also understand that it's not about me, and as I live my life based on the foundation of Christ, I can trust that He is for me and not against me. His ways are higher than my ways, and His favor will guide me perfectly in step with His plan. I don't need to fret or worry about one thing because I have committed the rest of my days to Him. He's a good Father, and nothing can stop whatever He has planned for my life or for yours!

When I say the word *butterfly*, you might picture a blue one or a black and white one or a yellow or green one. There are so many types of beautiful butterflies, but the point is that each one is uniquely different with its own markings and colors. I don't think I've ever sat around comparing them to one another; I simply fancy the pleasure of seeing them flit about, and I squeal with delight to be graced by their intricate, delicate beauty.

You and I are just like these butterflies. As we find our life in Christ, we've each been given unique traits, markings, colors, talents, and insights for great purpose in His kingdom. When you see yourself as He sees you, you will find your inspiration for joy and realize how you too can bring hope to others—because it isn't based on your vanity or insecurity; it is based in pure love. It is Christ in me who gives me wings to fly, strength to endure, and a broad band of colors to reflect His glory.

You might be wondering why all Christians don't always reflect the peace and harmony that Jesus brings. I believe that's because we are a work in progress, and we often lose our focus when we forget to pray and invest in the sweet fellowship that keeps us close to Him. God is so patient though, as He gently brings us back to center—where we learn to surrender and crucify the nature of our flesh. I can think of quite a few scenarios where I'd deal with people differently than He does, but that's what's so amazing about His grace!

When God's peace reigns within us, we are fully equipped to love others without judgment or fear, and we will not hurt others as much because we are less and less concerned about self-promotion or having control. When the mind of Christ operates in us, we become immune to the devil's lies and are essentially covered in Teflon so the enemy's attacks can no longer get a foothold in our thinking. It's a journey, it's a lifestyle, and it's a process, so be patient with yourself. He will graciously and mercifully lead you.

One of the most beautiful things about being reborn through Jesus is the experience of new grace. He fills us with a supernatural grace that not only goes beyond just saving us but also gives us the ability to rise above what might have previously kept us tethered to the ground. By His Spirit we become lighter than air and are unencumbered by external circumstances when our focus is on His resurrected life within us.

I can't tell you in how many situations His grace has proven to be sufficient for me, giving me the ability to rise above and conquer my own emotional response to them. This, my friend, is where true joy fills you, because you realize that without Him, there would be no way. Every day and every circumstance become an opportunity to see yourself as changed.

True survival won't sacrifice your purity on the altar of experience, and it doesn't exchange love and trust for bitterness and regret. Only Jesus can manifest the authentic survival of your whole being, because

He brings total restoration and resurrection to what seems dead and decayed. When we try to survive in our own abilities, we are limited to our selfish instincts or self-preservation to get us there. The end result is lackluster by comparison to what God offers us. Why would I trade having the absolute best and all the beauty of heaven for becoming a self-made copycat attempting to heal myself?

I would certainly never suggest that you forget to use the healthy God-given boundaries that wisdom and prudence require, but I am telling you that as you are healed from the wounds that would have otherwise destroyed you, you will have fresh mercy for others, including your abusers, and new discernment for breaking the chains that imprison those who are broken. In this way, you are equipped with the grace to lay down your own life, meaning the Bread of Life that Christ has given you, to lift up someone else. John 15:13 tells us, "Greater love has no one than this: to lay down one's life for one's friends."

In their book *The Elijah Task*, authors John and Paula Sanford shed a brilliant light on how this is done: "We often translate greater love has no man than that he should lay down his selfishness for his brother, or his ambition, or his own wishes. None of these things are life. They are death. We do not have life to lay down until we receive Christ's life. That is the life we are called to lay down."[14]

In my own life I have learned the joy and significance of laying down my life for someone else. What used to limit my ability to love others, especially those who treated me unjustly, was my focus on my need for love and my compound fear of rejection. But God has healed me so deeply that I am now able to make a conscious choice to immediately hand over what once would have offended me. If necessary, I take the pain of rejection to Him in my private prayer closet where we quickly settle the issue, and I'm overcome by the power of His Spirit and grace living within me.

Marriage is a good example of the kind of relationship that has the potential to either build you up or destroy you. When you've married your splendid opposite, the relationship is susceptible to contention on occasion because what once fueled your chemistry turns into the clanking sounds of iron sharpening iron. God intends to use your differences for good to build you both up, but be aware that the devil will try to use those differences and any unhealed wounds to harm you. This is why marriage can truly only work as intended when God is at the center of it—because true growth comes by laying down your lives for one another in the model of grace which Christ teaches us.

My husband and I both chose to apply this principle toward our marriage, understanding that it is by God's grace that we grow and become stronger as individuals and partners in love and life. The joy that comes from this act of divine love is inexplicable! This is where the threefold cord that is not easily broken comes into play (see Ecclesiastes 4:12). The reason for your strength is not found in your passion; it is found in the life of Christ within you. The third strand of the Holy Spirit is where you are empowered to lay down your life for your mate instead of wounding or judging them. It took me a long time to learn that I was inappropriately trying to be the Holy Spirit for other people and that love must always be the motive for any necessary correction, confrontation of truth, or prayer for personal growth, whether that be for myself or someone I have relationship with.

We all know that men and women are naturally wired quite differently in the way we process emotions and information. Likewise, friendships can have their differences too. This usually leaves room for misinterpretation of one another's intentions and hurt feelings or false judgments. When this occurs, I have learned to take my disputes to the Lord, and instead of complaining about my friend, family member, or husband, I bless them—because in God's presence, I can see them from Jesus' perspective and learn from the experience as well.

There is an interesting phenomenon that takes place when you bless someone in prayer. Fear loses its power over your mind and emotions when you align with God's heart and His Word. Even your greatest enemy must come under the authority of love when you place them before the Lord. In my experience, as I pray for my husband and loved ones, I speak complete restoration over their lives, and my love for them only deepens.

With regard to my own journey in marriage, this kind of unshakable love far surpasses the newness of amorous romance, because it is not based on my husband's performance or even his ability to get me all the time. This is a different kind of love than I've ever known. It has not only been tested over the years but also seasoned through prayer from our very first meeting. As I approach the throne of God with the anointing of Esther, He gives me peace, wisdom, and insight over the devil's agendas in any given situation. I am able to fight forward by the authority of the Holy Spirit, and no opposing voice can come against our divine purpose together, our marriage, our honor, or our destiny. When I leave the King's table, I am clothed with the substance of His glory and the power to walk in peace, love more deeply, serve more unselfishly, and hope more fully for those who cannot yet see what the Lord has done.

Being a believer does not mean you will get to skate through life without bruises. On the contrary, you have entered the battle zone on a whole new level, my friend, because there is purpose on your life. But this is only because you now have authority over the darkness that wanted to keep you, and the enemy is afraid of you, as you have been equipped to slay giants. Your enemy the devil conspires to use the things and people closest to you at times to try to throw you off your game or cause you to give up, but rest assured that when you find your identity in the holy of holies, nothing will stop you, and you will have the power to rise above each and every storm with the keen eye of an eagle.

Jesus said, "If you cling to your life, you will lose it; but if you give up your life for me, you will find it" (Matthew 10:39 NLT). This isn't a one-time choice; it is a daily one. How ludicrous would it be for the caterpillar to cling to its life because it just cannot imagine what it would be like to fly? Instead, it follows the divine call toward something greater, crawling upward until it can go no further, suspending itself in a tight cocoon as it waits for its promise in a meditative place of surrender.

Everything changes as it lays its life down for the new one that has been assured.

When we choose whom we will serve and what we will believe on a day-to-day basis, we grow from glory to glory. There have been many days where I failed to understand this, but I'm so thankful for the grace and mercy of God that gently guided me back into alignment with His heart. I grew closer and closer to Him simply because He loved me. This is why we needed a Savior and a Shepherd. It's the reason Jesus came to help us overcome. We are being perfected daily through His Word until we meet Him face-to-face, and in that, our process will feel much like the cocoon. It's the paradox of surrendering to love so that we might overcome like champions.

Selflessness requires a change of focus, which is the avenue where the power to bring down strongholds exists, but we usually don't recognize those strongholds that have occupied our thinking until we collide with the truth and recognize our desperate need for realignment. It's never easy or comfortable when doing so, and sometimes it's even quite painful as God straightens out what has grown with a crooked bent inside of us, but once we have been reset, we are able to grow past the ceiling of our old limitations. It's a little like having to reset a broken bone—painful for a short while but stronger and functional in the long term. It can take time for new truth to cement, but it surely will as you continue to place your hope and trust in Jesus. He is working on your behalf, advocating and interceding for us constantly.

When demonic strongholds are present in relationships, they feel toxic, but God wants to move through you to tear these strongholds down without harming the person you are in relationship with. The only way to do this is to learn the value of laying down your life for another. There have been many situations in my life that I wished were easier, but God equipped me with grace and showed me that He had assigned me to pray for that person because He trusted me to love them like no other ever had before. Sometimes you must love from a distance through prayer, which causes damage to the kingdom of darkness, forcing those strongholds to bow to the Name that is above every other name. Be patient in the process and learn to lovingly forgive just as Christ has done for you.

This requires us to step outside the perspective of ourselves to see from heaven's eyes. Would you believe that when you begin to see the people that hurt you as God sees them, it will set you free from every act of manipulation or intimidation they have ever used against you or any that you might have used against them? You'll actually have the strength to operate from within healthy boundaries while choosing to also love and extend kindness and compassion as your hope and trust lies in Jesus. The real definition of surrender isn't victimization; it is making a choice. It is handing over your whole heart and life to Christ so that, in exchange, you are equipped to lift up, edify, and bless the person who hates or opposes you.

If you don't have Christ's life at the center of your identity when those kinds of assaults come, you will feel threatened and revert to self-preservation mode instead of Christ-likeness. You can't serve others selfishly or with an agenda of your own. True service comes at a cost. God wants your light to shine, but not for your glory—it's for His. The reason for that is you cannot bring deliverance or healing to anyone in your flesh. The light within you is actually the glory of God drawing others to find their own life in Him too, because He *is love*! Once this understanding really sinks in, you will absolutely change your heart from desiring self-promotion to wanting all glory to go to God.

A good question to ask yourself is, "Am I a team player, or am I doing this for me?" Think for a moment about any area of your life where conflict can potentially arise. Relationship is what we were made for, first with God and second with one another, but too often our brokenness disrupts our unity. This principle applies to our ministries, our careers and work relationships, our church groups and activities, our families and our marriages, and to whatever role we play in the kingdom of God on earth. What are your motives for what you do at work, at home, or even in ministry? How would it effect you if you were to be promoted or demoted and replaced by someone else tomorrow with no recognition given for the work you've done? Have you surrendered all of your labor to the Lord? And are you doing everything as unto Him, or are you finding identity in your position?

It's easy to label what we do as for God, but the true test of our character is what lies at the root of our motive within our heart. Would you do the same thing if you received no credit or glory for what you do? Are you as faithful in the unseen things as you are under the watchful eye of people? We are so prone to forget that God sees us on a cellular level, and His value system is so different from ours. He looks upon our hearts, and Jesus said the servant would be the greatest in His kingdom (Matthew 23:11). It actually breaks my heart now to think of how long I sought to heal my own brokenness and fulfill my need for love with being seen, being noticed, being recognized, and being heard. I wore myself out trying too hard, but when Jesus fills your hunger with His love, it changes you and you no longer need to spend your energies chasing after attention. You just learn how to simply be, and the love inside you will flow out like a river.

Jesus warns us, "Be careful not to practice your righteousness in front of others to be seen by them. If you do, you will have no reward from your Father in heaven" (Matthew 6:1). He's not telling us that we are never to do anything publicly; He is confronting our motives for doing those good works. You will never walk in true power and authority until you relinquish all the glory to Him. I know from my own experience what a tragedy it is to have good fruit fall to waste simply because it was used for things God never assigned. You will spend all your energies untangling yourself from the mess you created and endure the criticism of others when this happens. When we seek His kingdom first and lay our lives down for others as He assigns us, we are promised that all those things we might have otherwise been concerned with will be added to us also.

If you really want to know your true purpose and value for being on this earth, it is to be the extended hands and feet of Jesus reaching to others. You are fully equipped to administer such healing and joy to your family, friends, and even strangers when you walk in sync with Him. When we are not self-driven, we are able to fulfill our divine purpose by giving our bread away to others, but we will never achieve the pure motives required or have enough bread to give without receiving it first from Christ Himself. He wants to dress you in the splendor of heaven, where even Solomon's riches cannot compare, and as you embrace the paradox of the King's table, the longings of your old life will float away like a distant memory on the wings of your resurrected one.

10

||||||||||||||||||||||||||

Building Strongholds
of Truth

I t was another long trip home from the East Coast in the aftermath of a crazy week's itinerary when our flight was suddenly cancelled due to inclement weather in Dallas, where we were supposed to catch a connecting flight to California. It was the night before my October birthday, and Paul and I had plans to spend it decompressing in Santa Barbara with dear friends, so staying overnight for an extra day wasn't exactly an option for us. Our only option was to book a different flight, and a journey that should have taken six hours collectively, took twelve hours from start to finish. Thankfully, we made the last flight out to Orange County, but our seat assignments were in separate rows due to the last-minute booking on a very full flight.

I was ready to hibernate in my window seat and work on some editing, but the Lord had different plans. As I sat there listening to concentration music through my earbuds, I could feel the lady next to me focusing her attention in my direction. I was quite tired and not in a talkative mood, so I kept reading through manuscript documents when she abruptly nudged me. As I looked over at her, I realized she wanted to say something, so I politely removed my earbud and said, "Yes?" Immediately, she engaged me in conversation over something meaningless, but before I could dismiss myself and return to my writing, she asked, "Are you writing a book?"

Noticing her countenance and communication skills, it became more obvious to me that she possessed a rather brilliant mind. Both she and her husband, who was sitting beside her, were rather laid-back and looked comfortable in their old-school hippie attire. They both carried thick reading materials and an air of intellectual superiority. Silently I conversed with God. *You know, I'm so tired and not really up to conversing with anyone right now, especially not someone who is going to challenge me either intellectually or about my views.* But immediately a peace came over my soul, and I *knew* God was asking me to reciprocate her inquisitiveness.

"Yes, I am." I smiled, anticipating the natural question that would follow. "Oh, marvelous," she responded, "and what is it about?"

"It's a book about identity and overcoming a victim mindset. I've inserted pieces of my own story to give an example of how I overcame abuse through the power of forgiveness." She was fascinated and wanted to know more. We chatted back and forth, and she immediately shared that she too had been sexually assaulted and how important the issue was to her, as well as to society on the whole. I listened compassionately and began to share about how my faith was the key to my personal healing. I started to sense that her tone was laced with a lack of comprehension.

As we continued to converse, I asked if she was a professor, and she acknowledged that she and her husband both had been university professors previously but at present, they were biotech engineers. Again, I whispered a prayer to God, who I believed had orchestrated this appointment. *Lord, I cannot begin to identify with this sweet woman on the same intellectual level, but I know you can compel her to the life and light that you have placed inside of me. Please give me the ability to listen to what she says and the right words to help her see a glimpse of you within me.*

This was during the height of the "Me Too" movement, just as the Kavanaugh hearings were winding down, and she adamantly spoke her mind about the issue of female victims needing to be heard. She passionately railed against "old white men" who want to rule our country with their outdated rhetoric, and I listened attentively, validating each one of her concerns. I then shared a broader perspective about the importance of truth and how there are many types of victimization in the world that have been witnessed throughout history. I spoke of wisdom and prudence to carefully check the facts and how we should never presume anyone guilty until proven innocent. She was level-headed and agreed with me about the need for compassionate, balanced treatment for all people.

"There is too much hate in our world," I continued to explain, "and hate will not fix anything. That is where the power of forgiveness changed my own victim mindset and identity."

She respectfully acknowledged my perspective and proceeded to explain hers. "I am not really a religious person, but from my experience with religious people, they tend to give God too much control or blame, saying it must have been His will that they go through what they did. The way I see it is they are using God as an escape from reality."

I agreed with her that this was a completely inaccurate assessment of the way God works and that perhaps she was correct about religion, by itself, being used as a means of denying reality. Then I said, "I view God's involvement from a completely opposite viewpoint! As a matter of fact, I realize now that He was the one who rescued me by pulling me out of a lifestyle that was killing me and gave me the faith to fight my own mindsets through the power of forgiveness."

She nodded with inquisitive eyes and then smiled as she leaned back in her seat, almost unsure of how to respond. We continued to make small talk about pharmaceuticals and rare genetic disorders, and I commended her for making a difference in this world. I wanted so badly to offer her a drink from my cup of faith, knowing that God loved her so much, but I knew better than to push. Perhaps I was merely to plant a seed—or water one that had already been planted by someone else. I continued to pray for that sweet, amazing woman who later wanted to meet my husband and gave a long wave and a smile as we went our separate ways just outside of the gate. I pray that she too will come to know Jesus personally and that He will transform her life with radiant joy from the inside out.

Everywhere you look today, people are trying to redefine truth and falsely pin the blame for the evils of this world on religion. Society says there is no identity in Christ and that true identity is fluid and based on who people *think* they are. They believe our identities can change, but what they don't realize is how much God has already accepted each of us individually for who He created us to be, and He loves us, despite the sin that has bound so many. He wants to see everyone free from that which enslaves and blinds them.

The church has also suffered from an identity crisis, partly because it has looked to culture for its relevance instead of finding the confidence to impact culture from its foundation in Christ. Once we truly understand who we are together, finding unity in Christ alone, we will be able to build a firm foundation of truth and fulfill our role as a unified body. We each have an individual role to play, but our corporate role is significantly impactful and can only be discovered through our identity in Jesus, the Bridegroom.

Truth in identity can only be based in God's Word, as He is the ultimate authority and our Creator. But there is a sobering effort happening around the world to remove God's Word from all secular fronts. This wave of antagonism suggests that the church has been wrong to believe in His infallible Word as the foundation for truth. This agenda seems to have leaked into the mindset of the modern-day church whether through rebellion or simply stemming from ignorance resulting from a lack of Bible consumption and knowledge. How can we call ourselves Christ followers if we don't even know what He says in His Word about the issues that are currently polarizing our culture?

It would seem that in the effort to rightfully combat religious abuse from the past, we have embraced a type of contempt for the Bible's call to holiness. The current hyper grace message gives the impression that we have an open license to sin without the need for Holy Spirit conviction because we have confused it with condemnation. God does not shame us. He awakens us to see what we cannot see or change without Him. What we've failed to realize is our human propensity to trade one system of religion for another as we shift our man-made boundary lines toward our comfort zones and contemporary ideals instead of searching for truth from a complete perspective of God's Word. He is the same yesterday, today, and forever; He will never change. Has our passion for Him been redefined or shaped by our emotional infatuation with the smoke and mirrors of our heavily produced worship encounters?

Before you tune me out, hear this: My husband and I are tremendous advocates and proponents of the power of media, and we love beautiful productions. We believe in good lighting and striving for excellence in everything we do so I don't say this judgmentally. I do believe, however, it's all too easy to lose sight of God in the constant hype about Him, and if we are not driven to worship Him in the quietness of our ordinary or difficult moments, we will miss the most precious opportunities to know Him more. Those are the places where we learn to hear His voice and become familiar with His heart. It is impossible to please Him without submerging your entire being in the identity of Christ where no one else can see you.

Our relationship with Jesus is a marriage, and every marriage needs constant work to keep the lines of communication open so that it can grow stronger behind the scenes of public affection. When we fail to nurture such a beautiful covenant relationship, it will become distant and grow cold, but when we invest ourselves, it becomes a reciprocating fulfillment between both partners. This is exactly what I believe the Scriptures are referring to when they talk about an adulterous generation. Israel is called out for its adulterous ways in Ezekiel 16, and Jesus again mentions an adulterous and wicked generation that seeks after signs when the Pharisees ask Him to produce one as a display of His power in

Matthew 12:38–39. It's all about the heart being fickle or uncommitted and our devotion to honor and love Christ as our bridegroom.

Imagine having a marriage where your partner never stops to consider you and never cares to just say I love you. Instead they focus their time and attention on other things or other people. Are we so busy in life that we are too busy to love God and make time for Him? When we are too busy to show our love and affection for Him daily, we usually have none to give to anyone else either, and I pray that the bride of Christ awakens to her first love again.

If we look at Newton's pendulum effect in his discussion of the laws of physics, he talks about the regular swinging motion caused by the opposing action of gravity. Any time an opposing motion presents itself, the pendulum swings to the other extreme, rocking back and forth in the balance. The church can sometimes resemble this same type of motion as its movements are caused by its beautiful diversity and the gravitational pull of God who also pushes back against the powers of darkness. Opinions and perspectives will always vary on theological, political, and relational issues, but when the body of Christ fully discovers its identity and value only in Him, it will also achieve the unity required to change the world. It's time that we move past our fears to embrace the peace of knowing that God is well at work within our midst and we are being perfected daily. The generations before us typically held tight to their standards of performance and legalistic views due to a fear based concept of salvation, but the current characteristics of the church display a lack of reverence or fear of the Lord in its relaxed perception of grace. Both stances are extreme expressions of the truth moving back and forth through the call of God, which lies in the balance where the pendulum reaches center and His gravitational pull draws us nearest to His heart. God is not neutral. He is the Alpha and Omega. The fullness of truth, purpose, and existence will always be discovered in Him.

I wonder how many Christian homes from past generations were filled with confusion as a result of religious abuse producing hypocrisy, condemnation, and performance instead of a genuine passion to honestly know God and become more like Him. We desperately need a new revelation of Jesus, and I believe He is standing on the horizon, ready to reveal Himself like we've never really known Him. First, we need to understand that our imaginings of who He is are vainly based in our lack of time spent with Him, and those imaginings must be subjected to His Word.

To be honest, most of the characteristics of Christ while He was here on earth are far from what we are inclined to pursue for our identities today! I am certain that Jesus didn't need to look in the mirror to reassure Himself by saying, "You are awesome, you have unlimited potential." He simply remained close to His Father in heaven, knowing exactly who He was in the Godhead. That is where He moved and breathed, doing nothing but what His Father told Him to do first, and so should we as we identify in covenant with Him.

Jesus found His significance in fulfilling God's Word by being the fulfillment of God's Word in the flesh. As His body and His bride, we are no different, because our closeness with the Father is what will encompass and equip us for greatness. We shouldn't have to pump up our flesh in order to gain confidence—that's where we get out of balance. We simply need a new revelation of who He is within us. The greater God's presence is within you, and the less you think about yourself, the more you will compassionately think of others and how to serve them.

Some of our carnal concepts and imaginings need to be cast down so that we can truly align with His power and identity. In chapter 5, I mentioned the example of casting everything that Queen Jezebel represented out from the window of our high towers. The apostle Paul puts it this way: "We are destroying sophisticated arguments and every exalted and proud thing that sets itself up against the [true] knowledge of God, and we are taking every thought and purpose captive to the obedience of Christ" (2 Corinthians 10:5 AMP).

We often misunderstand the free salvation of Jesus as something that just happens automatically when we accept Him as our Savior. What we fail to recognize is that part of accepting Jesus is following Him, not just in theory but with the utmost surrender of our hearts. Salvation is not limited to a one-time exchange during the "sinner's prayer"; it is a process of deliverance and renewal as we come to know Jesus and become like Him. Unfortunately, vain imaginings want to rule the mindsets of the world, but as believers, we are called to the highest standard of truth, which is God's infallible Word. And when we know truth intimately, it will set us free from our previous captivity.

Perhaps you realize that there are areas where you have been bound by arguments and philosophies that are exalted against the truth of God's Word. Bringing these areas under the authority of Christ is as simple as surrendering them to Him in prayer and receiving the mind of Christ by meditating on His life-giving Word. Even the idea of self-rejection is a vain imagining that must be cast down. The arguments that formerly breached the walls of your fortress will try to resurface through the enemy's lies, but your weapons against them and your tools for rebuilding a stronghold of truth will be found in the Bible. The book of Nehemiah paints the perfect picture of how we must build a new wall of protection from the foundation of God's Word so that we might defend and protect what God has revived.

This season of transition can feel much like you are doing double duty at times, wielding the sword against the enemy's warfare in one hand while tirelessly laying bricks and mortar with the other. Don't allow yourself to become discouraged or grow weary in "doing well" as you remain faithful to the call. You are rebuilding for future generations, and your obedience will be blessed for a thousand more, as God promises. Nehemiah was an amazing man anointed to lead God's people back to revival and restoration. He served as a cupbearer to the king, which was a very important position of high honor.

You, my friend, also have direct access to the King of kings, and, much like Nehemiah, you have been chosen to represent the kingdom of heaven, right here, right now. I encourage you to ask God for the wisdom to delegate the strategies necessary to rebuild whatever has been torn down in your life, your family, your marriage, your finances, or your church. You can and you will lead your children and children's children into revival if you keep your heart centered on what He has called you to do and not allow the voice of the enemy to intimidate you in this season. Truth must be fully restored if we want to be free from a life of powerlessness. There is no such thing as compromise when it comes to truth, and it may cost you everything. But as you embrace absolute truth as God has established it, you'll be cut loose from the lies that would have tethered you to the ground.

I believe the church is starved right now for more of God's power and glory. However, you cannot fill an old wine skin with new wine because once it is emptied of old wine, it becomes dry and brittle. Doing so would cause it to burst, because wine is a living, breathing, and evolving thing full of active enzymes (see Matthew 9:17). The same principle applies to the church. Our old systems no longer work because they've grown dry and brittle. Historically, the replacement of old wineskins meant preparing them for use again. The process required bathing or submerging them in water for a period of time and then oiling and massaging them so that the leather would become pliable again.

We are very much like the wineskins of old, needing to be reconditioned to receive whatever God wants to give us. There is a thirsty generation ready and waiting for new wine from the Holy Spirit, and they have come out of the religious rigidity of the past. The passionate heart in which they search for God has birthed a form of worship interestingly called "soaking." I'm not one to promote labels for anything, especially worship, but I find the draw for worship in this season to be fascinating. Deep worship is nothing new to me, as I have discovered intimate fellowship with Jesus in my own sanctuary for many years. It's a place where God and I commune and I meditate on the Word He speaks to me as I drink from His cup. I believe the younger generation is instinctively searching for something new, and we are about to see His Spirit poured out on the young and the old.

No better portrait of softening exists than the bride of Christ soaking in the water of the Word of God and drinking in His presence. To achieve that kind of renewal, we must allow the freedom of the Holy Spirit to anoint us with oil as He gently massages the parts of us that have become calloused. We must be tenderized so that we can be useful again and connected to His voice. We aren't meant to remain strictly in the soaking place—we'd become useless and bloated if that were the case. God wants to repurpose and reform us back into His perfect image so that His truth can flow from us freely and joyfully. This is how we will ignite a fire on this earth that will change it.

A truly redefined identity can only be found in the origin of Christ and should be sought within the spectrum of church government and those in leadership. Before leaders can truly feed and equip their people to be the eunuchs and Jehus that will effectively cast down the lies that have come against the purity of our worship, they must recalibrate their own hearts first. The overflowing glory and joy that comes from new life is a contagious force meant to heal and restore others to their fitted place in the kingdom.

We mustn't forget that sickness (death) and rebellion are contagious too. They are usually masked in goodness as they creep into our hearts. It's time to stop worrying so much about only building our platforms and church attendance and start focusing on the Life Builder so that we have the power and grace to truly love others, without selfish agenda attached to our service. As we build these strongholds of truth, the hungry and malnourished will come and be filled at the authentic table of the King, where the bread of life never runs out and they will be changed forever.

We mustn't forget that God rescued us after He found us kicking in our own natal blood (Ezekiel 16:6). Just as He commanded us to live then, we must continue to heed the call now. The development of our spiritual and emotional growth changes us, but without a continual divine revelation of our hope in Christ alone, we will forget what we came from and end up following the example of Israel in the book of Ezekiel. Israel broke the heart of God as she wandered away in her arrogance and adulterous practices, forgetting that He had rescued her in her infancy. What a tragedy to be found prostituting what God has given us for our own gain instead of using it to bring others into the presence of His glory.

The stronghold of truth that has held many generations together has nearly been demolished by the pressures of culture today. Our lack of spiritual insight and laziness has made us slaves instead of conquerors. If we're going to rebuild, we must make disciples of people by encouraging their identity in Christ alone and addressing the abuse, emotional wounds, and pride that have hijacked so many of them. It is pertinent that the church realizes the value of carefully constructed counseling programs as essential to the healing of souls that have been wounded. Then those wounded healers can be fully equipped for kingdom purpose and advancement.

Marriages, families, and singles are desperate for help with the challenges they face in today's society, and it's our job to give them the help they need. As the sheep heal and are transformed by the newness of Christ, the church will automatically grow through their evangelism, and so will their monetary giving. We have erred in our fear-based ministries as we've forgotten the real purpose for what we do when numbers and dollars become the primary goal. Once the focus is on restoring identity for the body of Christ, the necessary provisions will come because God wants us healing the hurting and making a real difference. He will provide what we need to do so, without a doubt. It's a heart issue that needs fixing—not a money problem. In the next chapter we'll take a look at the corporate power tools that we can use together to change this hurting world.

There is something coming straight from heaven for those who have been prepared. It won't matter how long you have or have not known Him or how long you have or have not served in your ministry. If you've been through things that nearly destroyed you but survived in the person of Jesus Christ, you are a part of His remnant and the vessels that He is going to use to pour out His glory in these days. Stand ready and faithful as we heed the call to change the atmosphere of darkness with faith, hope, and love!

11

|||||||||||||||||||||||||||||

Stop Hurting
and Help People Heal

An accurate portrayal of the church is really only possible when it's seen through the eyes and perception of Christ. The divine depiction of His bride is fully established in her solitary immersion with the Bridegroom. Becoming one by His blood, He equips her to do even greater things than He did on earth. It is a beautiful impression that is yet to be fully witnessed and far from what the world has seen through its lens of criticism. She is a perfect vision in white, radiantly dressed in His glory, and the role she plays is a significant one for such a time as this.

Although historically she has failed time and again to represent the fullness of the kingdom of God, much of her beauty comes from the fact that her humanity is redeemable by God's grace. Throughout the ages, the church has persevered through tremendous persecution and thrived under tyranny. It has endured many sufferings throughout the generations, some due to a gross lack of knowledge about God's ways, but the body of Christ is continually being perfected in grace as it grows from age to age and from glory to glory. There are greater things to be done as He perfects His image of love within us. God has promised that the gates of hell will not prevail against the church and that Jesus is returning for a spotless bride without even a wrinkle on her garment.

Wrinkles in clothing result from sitting or sleeping in them, and I am convinced that God is shaking things up to awaken and reposition His people, calling those who will listen to be transformed in this hour, because we have work to do. The role of the church is to be Christ's body to the world and nothing more, nothing less. Jesus' goal was to heal, deliver, and transform, and He wasn't afraid of what people looked like in their sin. Nor did he try to become like them to gain popularity or influence. His embrace was one of compassion to feed, heal, speak truth, and restore dignity wherever it was needed. He had the ability to see beyond the cloak of religiosity and the posture of brokenness because He was able to value and esteem the spirit and soul of a person, seeing them all along for who they were created to be.

In the words of the great Oswald Chambers taken from "Sacred Service":

> The Christian worker has to be a sacred "go-between." He must be so closely identified with his Lord and the reality of His redemption that Christ can continually bring His creating life through him"...

> "If we simply preach the effects of redemption in the human life instead of the revealed, divine truth regarding Jesus Himself, the result is not new birth in those who listen. The result is a refined religious lifestyle, and the Spirit of God cannot witness to it because such preaching is in a realm other than His. We must make sure that we are living in such harmony with God that as we

proclaim His truth He can create in others those
things, which He alone can do."[15]

How unfortunate it is and how it must break the heart of God when
people come to church hungry, but instead of finding the Jesus who will
break their chains, they find a message about how to be relevant and
how to affirm yourself or perhaps a room full of people who are merely
seeking social cliques or, worse yet, are still identifying with and relating
through their wounds, victimization, and offenses. Of course, none of us
are perfect, and we are all in different places of spiritual growth, because
we are a work in progress. My point is not intended to criticize the body
of Christ; it is to awaken her for greater purpose through the healing
identity of Jesus, which sets us free from ourselves.

The church assembly is not a platform for our selfish ambitions; it
is a house of healing and empowerment. Unless we truly heal our own
wounds in the identity of Christ, we cannot create the necessary atmosphere for miracles to take place or be the healing hands that the world
so desperately needs. We have become stuck in our issues, making them
the platforms of our ministries and believing we can speak life from our
unhealed wounds by merely using God's name. But our message will
remain powerless until we move past identifying with our issues and
fully embrace who we are in Christ. You were meant to radically change
the world through your love—not remain a part of its broken ideology.

If we don't choose to leave our old identity behind and find our new
one in the freedom Christ offers, we remain performers and hypocrites
of the heart and will continue to lack compassion for those who are
defeated and bound by their blatant strongholds. When leaders abuse
their power by forgetting to show genuine compassion to those who
desperately need Jesus, they become instruments of more rejection and
destruction instead of messengers of hope. Leaders who have not truly
realized their own human propensity to deny Christ, like Peter did, tend
to puff themselves up with an incorrect interpretation of the Word and
false humility. This is where we easily derail from God's original intent

for us by solely focusing on alignment with like-minded people to build our churches. In my opinion, this is often the source of segregation and division in church congregations.

I truly don't believe that most church pastors or leaders in ministry start out with the wrong motivation. I think they lose their way, so to speak, by becoming consumed with ministry instead of Jesus first. It is a human tendency to want to build and protect the empires we birth, but unless God builds the house, we labor in vain. We cannot produce Christ-likeness without daily fellowship with Him to fill our cup with His love and acceptance. As a former victim of abuse and brokenness, I can't say enough about how wonderful it was when a pastor or leader truly saw me and valued me as a child of God instead of categorizing me and treating me as shameful. To be honest, I've been treated both ways, but unfortunately it was mostly the latter.

I often felt intimidated, misjudged, dismissed, or abandoned at work or church because it had become a part of my mental makeup. This frustrated me to no end, but I didn't realize I could change it with the right mindsets and behaviors. People who are broken, awkward, ashamed, and unknowledgeable need to be mentored in love and discipline so that they can learn to thrive as wounded warriors who know how to strategize against the enemy—not only for themselves but for others in their future as well.

I often just put on a brave face in church settings whenever it felt unsafe to be honest and vulnerable. I desperately needed a place of safety to be heard and healed, but because I was good at hiding my painful flaws, I gave the illusion that I was well put-together. They usually rushed to welcome me but later rejected the internal deficit that eventually became recognizable. Rather than helping me heal more quickly by addressing my issues with truth and love, they subtly heaped on more shame by socially dismissing me. Wounded people are perceptive and highly aware when they have been demeaned, regardless of their education or social status.

The worst place for these dehumanizing dynamics is in the church.

Impatience, criticism, and bad advice can become borderline spiritual abuse. I naively trusted people who I considered to be spiritual leaders in my life, but because of my upbringing, I ignorantly chose to give them the authority to control me. It was my natural bent and the way I showed respect and honor to these individuals, but eventually God had to teach me that my need for approval and the church leaders themselves were not to be my idols.

Some of the pastoral counseling I received was a derivative of their legalistic reasoning that wasn't based on divine discernment. I was often encouraged to submit to my abusive husband instead of exploring the deeper issues attached to abuse and didn't receive the help and support that I needed to find safety and healing. Please hear me when I say that I am not angry at the church in any way! I understand how huge the problems that affect our culture are and how overwhelming it can be for leaders to balance all aspects of church ministry and growth. I simply feel I can give some insight to those who haven't come from such a broken background and don't know how to relate to abuse survivors.

For so long I concealed the evidence of abuse that was taking place at home in order to protect the image of my marriage at church. Then later when the truth was revealed, I was shunned and my life began to fall apart. The pain of such betrayal, when your life is in ruins, runs even deeper than the scars or bruises from spousal abuse. These wounds are the Judas kiss, coming from those who had the power to protect and comfort but chose to turn away in embarrassment or disbelief instead.

Spiritual abuse of power is not acceptable, and it has caused many people to turn away from the church as a safe harbor. I've heard my husband say that the church should be a hospital for the hurting, but it is often perceived as a courtroom. If the church is filled with a prideful religious spirit instead of the spirit of love, it will not produce the life change needed in those who want to be healed. Instead it will produce judgment and condemnation. It is critical that we equip people properly and train them for more than just how to be ushers. A full-time Christian is a full-time minister, and they are hungry to know how to effectively represent the kingdom in the ministry they have been called to, whether in the church or in the workplace.

Through the ages, God's role for women in the church has been demeaned and downplayed due to poor interpretation of Scriptures that were originally written as letters to address specific situations in specific churches by the apostle Paul. Superimposing what God intended to be admonition for specific issues in a single church as a universal standard for the whole church doesn't make sense. This is another deceptive assault sent from the enemy to keep women and men from becoming who they were created to be in the corporate body. Remember that we were also taught in the book of Galatians, that in Christ there is no male or female, no Greek or Jew, which we will discuss more in the next chapter. We are one in body, and our anointing is greater through our unity. This form of intimidation toward women has crippled the church's effectiveness on the whole, and ironically it has sabotaged men by restraining a part of their own body that God intended to use against the enemy's forces of destruction. Women mattered to Jesus when He walked on the earth, and they matter to Him still today. They were created for influence and purpose, not to be demeaned or gagged and bound as useless creatures made only for the pleasures of men.

Women who truly love Jesus will give birth to things and walk in a divine discernment and graceful honor that is valuable to the kingdom. They are gifted healers and warriors against powers of darkness, but they have been marginalized and over-sexualized by those who are operating in their own brokenness and fear. The assault on women started in the garden of Eden when Eve's curse set the world as we know it today in motion. The blood of Jesus has broken that curse, and it's time we let go of fear on all sides, submitting ourselves to the authority of Christ. Only then can we truthfully work together in unity, honoring one another as a body of saints who is empowered to reign in dominion over the earth. A true body flows in its God-given abilities and comprehends when to remain stationary and when to move.

For example: When I type on my computer, my brain commands

each hand to flow in its skilled synchronization. Amazingly, this machine called the human body works in conjunction with my mind and my hands to create substance. But when it's time to pick up my coffee cup, just my right hand receives that memo, because it is the strongest and most coordinated for the task. Now wouldn't it be silly for my left hand to get jealous and begin fighting or undermining my right hand in either scenario? Likewise, we must see ourselves as complimentary parts of a body rather than independently rebelling against one another. We cannot flow in unity unless we flow in the love and identity of Christ.

Church leaders are as human as their flocks and vulnerable to the same attacks from the enemy, if not worse. They are targeted because of their role as influencers and teachers of God's people, which is all the more reason why every leader should run to Jesus for spiritual refreshing, grace, and wisdom on a daily basis. God's wisdom results in loving boundaries that produce the healthy environment required for unity to thrive. Unity is not a meshing together of codependent identities; it is a harmonious togetherness that celebrates differences and creates balance and synergetic results under the love and authority of Christ.

The key here is that Jesus is the superpower that flows through us, and He alone brings us to the love and acceptance that we all desperately need. But when we are filled with idolatry, we hurt each other instead of healing one another. The enemy knows that he can keep us defeated by secretly enslaving leaders in burnout, depression, and sexual addiction until shame can drive them to live double lives, reducing their passion for ministry to drudgery.

When leaders are attacked, the sheep are then left unprotected and unequipped. The devil wants to propagate the same lie that removed him from heaven by keeping people focused on the struggle for power and control. He brings accusations against brothers and sisters to destroy them, and if we are not operating in love, defensive manipulation will reign instead. It's our job as the church to recognize these strategies and make war on the kingdom of darkness that has held the church hostage for too long.

Leaders can change their tendency toward inadvertent spiritual abuse by proactively equipping the identity-wounded body for kingdom purpose. This shift will manifest through prayer and humility, as it begins with healing the leaders first. Many have become the sacrificial lambs they were never intended to be, overworking themselves (as much as seventy-five hours per week) until their personal relationships with family start to suffer. The enemy is afraid of what he knows the church will soon become, and so many men of God have been targeted where they are most vulnerable, resulting in stress-related sickness, depression, and addiction invading their lives. Perhaps not surprisingly, the statistics for pastors suffering from burnout, crisis, and/or sexual addiction are extremely high today. But I'm here to encourage you that what the enemy has meant for your harm will be turned and used for good if you'll step into the light and love of Jesus. Only He can transform your heart and make it new again.

As a church or ministry leader, you are valuable to the kingdom. Don't allow your destiny to be robbed; find your true power and authority to be effective in what you are called to do. In order to heal, you must face your failure and the pressure to perform so that you can become authentic. This is your Simon-Peter moment. Most ministers feel they must cover up or protect their reputation, for fear that people will leave and they will lose tithing support. But that is a burden that God wants to carry for you. It was never intended for the leadership to carry this kind of weight. Our only commission is to love and to believe.

As we turn our cares over to the Lord and risk it all, essentially losing our life (even in ministry), the Bible promises we will find it (Matthew 10:39). From this place we can learn to share from our own broken experiences so that others will truly see the Christ who redeemed us and set us free, giving hope to the hopeless! There is no such thing as burnout in the kingdom of God. When we walk in His divine anointing and empowerment, His yoke is an easy one and His burden is light because there is joy instead of resentment when we truly see God moving through us. We are called to fight the good fight but not become overwhelmed by the impossible load that we place upon ourselves or by those we allow to be inappropriately placed upon us. If you are a pastor or church leader and you're dealing with dangerous burnout, I encourage you to go back to your Source and get honest with God.

You cannot give what you do not already possess, and if your storehouse is empty, you need some time alone with God to recalibrate and place your burdens, including your sin, upon the Rock of ages. The deception of the enemy would have you believe that the success of your ministry is up to you, but that is a lie rooted in rebellion, which will only bring death to the sheep you feed as well as to your own household. As you remove your self-driven identity from your service in the kingdom and tap the wellspring of Christ within you, you will do great exploits and people's lives will be changed for eternity.

It is equally important as leaders that we operate in the wisdom of healthy boundaries. Understanding when God is asking us to stop and give our attention to a situation or person that we think we don't have time for can be confusing. Jesus is our example, and we frequently read accounts in the Scriptures where He broke away from the crowds after a long day of ministry to pray in the surrounding hills. Notice He wasn't at the golf course or fishing on the lake, which is quite alright. He was intentional to find a place of seclusion where He could be restored and hear the voice of His Father with clarity. When Jesus recognized His own need to refill His cup, He took the opportunity to do so! I'm not being a religious prude on this, and I do believe Jesus enjoyed life and also cared about building His relationships by having fun with those He loved, but He didn't choose them over His Father when it came to feeding and rejuvenating His Spirit, soul, and body.

I admonish myself first and foremost on this subject more than anyone else, knowing the type of exhaustion that comes with spending so much time pouring out spiritual encouragement to others and meeting demands. Even studying the Word can become a redundant task when it's routine and without hunger to hear what the Sprit is saying. The temptation to fill one's cup with other inferior replacements should never take precedence over our time spent in private prayer and worship. Please understand that I do believe in restoration of the human psyche and physical body through fellowship and recreation. It's extremely important, but I also think we must be very intentional about guarding the most important element of our existence and identity: time with our Father God in covenant communion.

Discipline and natural talent are wonderful gifts when they're used for excellence, but no amount of either will ever replace the work of the Holy Spirit in our ministries. What we must not forget is that while we walk in grace for our salvation, passivity in our spiritual requirements will not yield the results we need. We are partners with God, and our strength and anointing will always be found in our fellowship with Him. That is where honesty in His presence will take us each and every time. God told Zerubbabel in Zechariah 4:6, "Not by might nor by power, but by my Spirit, says the LORD Almighty." Zerubbabel was a governor in the Persian Province of Judah, who, together with the high priest, Joshua, led the first wave of Jewish returnees from exile and began to rebuild the temple. God is calling you to the same today as you stand with your High Priest, Jesus, to lead God's people back to the land of promise and the place of true worship.

As ministers of the gospel and members of the body of Christ, it's important that we readily forgive any person operating in a spirit of offense. This is a sensitive season riddled with polarized political views and an increasingly volatile climate that has affected the entire world. We have an opportunity right in front of us to restore love, unity, and a vision of hope through Christ. We need to repent to one another for the acts of unkindness that have been committed, even by the generations before us. It will be essential to maintain a heart of forgiveness and love for those who have spoken against us with false accusations or harmful intent in this hour. This type of mercy and grace can only come from the Christ within you, but He wants to equip you to do the impossible so that we can usher in a true revival.

This is crucial when you've been caught in friendly fire because of the enemy's accusations against you. God can seem silent when an accuser is running rampant among us, but we must seek Him even harder in those challenging times instead of dwelling on the injustice. I have wept bitterly, asking God, "Where is your justice? Where is your vengeance for those who have been wrongly accused or displaced and forgotten through the manipulation of demonic agendas?"

My husband and I both have been tested to the core in this area, and what I've come to discern is that when God wants to bring strongholds down in families, churches, ministries, and even nations, the enemy works his hardest to prevent our victory through the roadblock of offense! There is no way out of these spiritual death traps other than by God's grace, and I assure you that His grace only comes when we completely surrender our need to Him and His timing. Being a seer and prophetic in spirit, I have a tendency to loathe manipulation and dishonesty when I see it operating on deeply hidden levels. However, my heart has been conditioned to wait upon the Lord so that my gifts will only be used to heal and not hurt others. Vengeance and justice belong to Him alone.

I think we've reached a crossroads in the church today. As global social and economic pressures mount, we must search our own hearts and ask God to cleanse them so that we have divine direction for how to move forward from here. What are you consumed with and what inspires you? Is the example of Jesus what fuels your spirit, or are you caught up in conforming to the world's culture? It's enticing to build our programs and outreaches with cultural appeal simply to grow church numbers, but this is not the key to reaching people. The key to drawing the hungry in is to offer them solid food! Our programs need to center around the burgeoning needs of our congregations and communities. Those initiatives will most likely look different in each community, but the common denominator between us all is the hope we give through the gospel of Jesus Christ.

Instead of waiting for the government to implement change, we must be the change, recognizing our unique position and divine responsibility to truly help the hurting come out of their bondage. As I mentioned earlier, it may require forgiveness and better boundaries to find a new approach to loving the sheep that God gives you. There are people who have come out of deep brokenness and are ready to serve as the wounded healers the world desperately needs. Their scars will be testimonies of God's grace and forgiveness, and they will know how to bandage the open wounds of others better than it's been done traditionally.

It's time to heal so many injustices where people feel they are not being heard. Women and minority groups need to be fully restored and valued in the body. Children who have been forgotten need to be taken in and covered. Victims of abuse need to be heard, healed, and empowered with a new identity. There is a host of orphaned souls that need to find a home and enough injustices in the world to keep every church busy spreading the healing hope of Christ. If we can shift what consumes our platform ministries into pouring as much or more time, money, and resources into correcting real injustices through counseling and rehabilitation programs, along with equipping ministers with the tools they need, we will change the world.

We're at a turning point where many injustices and abuses toward other human beings have robbed generations of the ability to love again. God is calling you to love beyond an emotion. He is calling you as His remnant bride to keep your lamps burning strong so that you will be anointed and empowered with the wisdom and grace to bridge the gap of our cultural, physical, emotional, and spiritual differences. He is equipping you to apply the salve of love and truth to the wounds and injustices that have bound too many to a lie. I believe this is the generation in which the church will rise up in its true power and authority to break those chains of deception and turn what was meant for devastation into a beacon of hope for the good of all humanity. In the next chapter we'll talk about the greatest power tool we can use to fulfill this honorable call as a corporate body of believers.

12

‖‖‖‖‖‖‖‖‖‖‖‖‖‖‖‖‖‖‖

The Color of Love

As an artisan by trade, for many years my strong suit was analyzing and understanding color and composition. This made me a very successful liaison for paint stores and clients needing my consulting advice for wall colors and textiles. Art and color have a unique way of speaking to us, and just as we're made up of body, soul, and spirit, color also reflects the glory of the Godhead as it consists of three primary components: pigment, binder, and solvent. There are also only three basic primary colors, from which all other colors are derived: red, yellow, and blue.

Being a lover of truth and authenticity, I was passionate about replicating as closely as possible the color pallets in nature that I drew inspiration from. However, I'm not a purist when it comes to design; I love the power of juxtaposition and muted tones. Like nature, the human experience is a complex sum of struggles and genetics that produces unique results every time. The element of surprise keeps things interesting, and perhaps even lends itself to our effectiveness in the kingdom. God said He would use the foolish and abased things of this world to confound the wise—not the perfectly polished and panache who appear to have never been stained or tinted with compromise. Let that sink in if your journey has led you to believe you have nothing to offer Him.

In the history of the world, the color red has held both religious and secular connotations. It represents the color of beauty, passion, boldness, lust, and love, but its chief representation is of Jesus' blood, which required unprecedented love in order for it to be shed as the sacrifice for a lost world. By divine inspiration, all the colors blend in a synchronized order to create a rainbow, which is God's original sign of promise. When I look at a rainbow, I see the reflection of the Godhead. Red represents the blood of Jesus, the Son, which connects us to the Father, who is light and represented by the color yellow. Blue is the color of the heavens and water—a calming presence like the Holy Spirit, who was sent to be our comforter, counselor, and guide.

What a gorgeous story that's told in the composition of a rainbow about the promise of God's love for each and every one of us! The enemy has tried to hijack that symbol to represent a counterfeit of love, but we need to remember that within the very structure of its glowing hues is the foundation of triune truth! We were created to enjoy color, and what we see here on earth is only a fraction of what we will see in heaven. How is it then that we get so hung up on color when it comes to our skin? We are all just reflections of something bigger than us, but the enemy has tried to tear us apart by sowing dissention in the human race.

We live in a culture that celebrates individualism instead of unity, tribalism instead of identity in Christ, and we are divided because of deception. The inhumane treatment of people throughout history, and even today, is an atrocity to God. Without a transformation of the heart through identity in Christ, we will not have enough grace and love to change the tide, but I believe there is a remnant of people who have come through devastation and the enemy's attacks as pure gold, ready to be the change we have so desperately needed.

The apostle Paul wrote, "There is neither Jew nor Gentile, neither slave nor free, nor is there male and female, for you are all one in Christ

Jesus" (Galatians 3:28). It is time for those who identify with Christ to rise up and fight for all of humanity and for the church, as God has called us to. Perhaps what you've considered to be your identity is something God wants you to rise above so that, by His grace, you will no longer be tied to what has limited you. Together we will break dividing walls and fight for justice by eliminating division first within our places of worship. When true repentance, forgiveness, and love take place, we will see the fruit of unity, and nothing will stop us. Not even the gates of hell can prevail against the remnant body of Christ.

Part of our division has manifest between men and women, and both sexes have deeply hurt one another through selfishness and mistrust. God gave both men and women vital roles within the church and commissioned them to have dominion over the earth and to replenish it. There are many ways that we can be fruitful and multiply in this day and age, but we need each other to do so. Where one person can only set a thousand to flight, two can create the synergy to set ten thousand to flight by joining forces and recognizing shared values.

Competition between the sexes originated with blame when the serpent deceived both Adam and Eve, hijacking their true identities and hiding them from both God and one another. He did so by lying and then pitting them against each other in condemnation and fear. He is the accuser of the brethren and still uses the same tactics today to keep us from having power over him. God wants us to live in harmony, and collectively we bring tools to the corporate table such as our talents and spiritual gifts that work in sync to effectively fulfill God's purposes.

Love is not lust. We all know that, but it's still easy to confuse the two when you lack identity and struggle for significance or power. This issue has not only overshadowed secular society but also invaded the church, where culture has become a primary source of inspiration. If we're more concerned with creating or following a brand and more consumed with what we are wearing than how well we are fulfilling the unselfish love of Christ toward others, we are trapped in a false mindset and our hearts have been grossly deceived. The lust of the eye, lust of the flesh, and pride all, unfortunately, steer the hearts and minds of so many believers who only cherry-pick convenient parts of the gospel to fulfill their personal agendas.

It is absolutely okay to look good and present yourself as best you can and as Christians, we should be reflecting the excellence of God in all of our attributes. Life and ministry should also be fun, and they will be when love is the motivation behind everything we do. Joy is our God-given reward when we choose to live beyond ourselves. Unfortunately, today's culture reinforces and encourages an unhealthy projection of image, and while it's important to take care of our bodies, which are the temple of the Holy Spirit, we also need to understand that self-love is not the same as narcissism. It's actually quite the opposite. Narcissism is rooted in self-rejection, which is the driving force behind a false identity.

When we see ourselves as Christ sees us and learn to appreciate whom we were created to be, we gain a healthy love for ourselves that doesn't require seeking out acceptance from people. Self-rejection, or the hatred of one's true person, is very painful, and if it's not healed in the presence of God, it will cause victims to project a persona in a pathetic cover-up or counterfeit identity. If you are constantly chasing the endorphin rush of approval or befriending high-profile people simply to improve your own image, you might search your heart for what's driving you. In a world that now centers on social media, are you disconnected from the real-life assignments God might be calling you to? Do you drop real friends for those with more *followers* or do you let the Spirit of God lead and assign you to relationships that will produce more eternal value, even when it hurts?

If you are consumed with how well you are received, you are most likely missing the opportunities that God is placing before you. We cannot hear His voice if we are too busy listening to the noise of public opinion through the distraction of our devices. The point is that whatever you choose to identify with is going to shape your identity and drive you either toward or away from your divine purpose. Even racial identity (regardless of which color one's skin is) is a tribal mentality, but when we follow after Jesus, we are no longer identified by the race we were born into. We are now a kingdom race, perfectly fitted into the body of Christ for His purposes, not our own. This is not to say that we were not made male or female, or to deny that we're given a variety of skin tones by divine design. Rather, this emphasis on no gender or race is simply a new paradigm for how we are to treat one another in the kingdom of heaven on earth. It is a way to say, "I'm no longer thinking about myself and my rights. Instead, I am God-conscious and ready to fulfill whatever He would ask of me."

Racial reconciliation is an urgent need in society, but it's going to require obedience from the church before we can effectively initiate healing for the world. Love runs red from the cross of Jesus! Scripture tells us in 1 Peter 4:8 that "love covers over a multitude of sins," which means it's a necessity for those offenses that seem impossible to forgive.

Love is not a warm and fuzzy feeling nor is it as simple as the lyrics to a Beatles song. Love is a choice that must be governed by the truth of God's Word and that kind of true love will only flow from our lives as an example of Christ who is seated at the helm of our identity. When Christ is at the center of our identity, our hearts change. He miraculously turns our fear and prejudice into compassion and honor for one another. We can't have a heart for the nations without encountering His transforming love first!

In his brilliant book, *The Truth in Black and White,* Bishop Harry Jackson states:

> Our Christian faith demands that we look past hurts and resentment and find new ways to work together in order to preserve the values we hold dear. That, I believe, is the foundation of a new paradigm and a model for political realignment that can transform our world. But, more importantly, it is the biblical paradigm for a dynamic

faith that calls all God's children to live and work
together in one accord for the common good.[16]

When we fail to speak the truth of God's Word to others as it applies
to our common issues, we are actually withholding the key to freedom
and fulfillment from them because of our selfish regard to our own comfort, forgetting the importance of the welfare and salvation of another
human being. Learning to love requires effort and diligence, as we are
following the model of Christ's love, which is a significant part of the
process of change. This is how we start the conversations that will heal
us.

When love comes alive in you, it will empower you to lay down
your own life, your own agenda, and often your own will for the sake of
another. This is what submission is about. It is not meant to constitute
abuse or domination. It is meant to empower the giver with grace so
that the other person's heart might be softened and pierced with life-
changing truth. Husbands and wives are commissioned to submit to one
another, but love, grace, honor, and respect are key to successfully building a healthy marriage covenant. Divorce is not the ultimate answer for
irreconcilable differences; love is. God can redeem what the enemy has
stolen through the obedience of two people, which usually begins with
the obedience of one. Stop labeling your spouse, your child, or even
yourself, and start prophesying what love says about them. Love doesn't
give up—it is faith-filled and it never fails (see 1 Corinthians 13). If God
releases you from something that is demonically destroying you, you will
know it by His confirming Word and His peace, but I strongly caution
you to allow the Holy Spirit to examine your heart in the process, as love
alone must guide you to victory.

Love believes all good things and calls into being things that were not!
That is our promise if we choose to have faith by grace as Abraham's off-
spring. Against all hope, Abraham believed God's plan for his life and
became the father of many nations, just as God had vowed. It's important
to follow his example of unwavering faith and belief so that we too will be

strengthened spiritually, physically, and emotionally (Romans 4:16–22). Can you *call into being* the promise or divine nature that you perceive God has purposed in someone else even when it is not yet evident in his or her behaviors? This is what Jesus did with the woman at the well. Society looks at us and sees our dirt, saying, "Oh, I know *who* you are!" But Jesus looks at us and sees the treasure buried deep in our soil, which He bought and paid for with His life, and He calls it forth saying, "I know who *you* are!" He separates our "do" from our "who." In other words, He doesn't equate our value with what we have done whether by works or by fault. He crowns us with dignity because of who we are as God's ultimate and beloved creation. This is the example He asks us to follow when He said, "This is My commandment, that you love one another as I have loved you" (John 15:12 NKJV). He wants us to do the same as we view people through the prophetic lens of His love and compassion.

When we truly get a revelation of this principle, we will stop allowing the enemy to rule over our emotional triggers and our relationships. We can then recognize and rise above the demonic chaos that is sent to destroy us and begin to speak truth and healing with the authority of God's love instead. This is the most beautiful application of prophecy in my opinion. We must ask the Holy Spirit to help us see one another as He sees us because perfect love casts away all fear. And when fear is removed, we are no longer triggered by it and instead able to finally reach across the gap of deception, bitterness, manipulation, and intimidation just as Jesus did to build a bridge on the altar of holy sacrifice.

In this day and age we overemphasize the power of secular knowledge and information while de-emphasizing the rightful study of God's Word, which often leads us to take matters of injustice into our own hands, processing them strictly according to our emotions. This is not the answer to freedom or advancement. Merely being *right* is futile and only adds fuel to a raging fire. If we want to be healed and restored to dignity, we will only see it manifest through our submission to God and His love poured out from our surrendered spirits to those who have injured us. This is a place where skin color doesn't matter, offenses lose their power over us, and there is joy in celebrating our uniqueness and our oneness in Christ. If you have been greatly wronged, God has plans to greatly use you to usher this kind of forgiveness and healing into a broken system. His Word and His ways never change.

As a woman, it may feel like I am living in a man's world at times, but that is not my barometer for truth, because in Christ I can do all things. I am not limited by this world's definition of what a woman is, nor am I limited by any man's opinion or treatment of me as I follow Christ wholly and completely. In my healing, I have learned to rise above the opposition, which came from the curse of sin, to become the hands, feet, and mouthpiece of God's love. God is no respecter of persons; He is an equal opportunity God. As long as I have submitted my will to Him and have stopped seeking after my own idols, His favor is mine. He is the Alpha and the Omega, He knows the end from the beginning, and all life has come from and through Him. His entire purpose for creating us was to have relationship with us and for us to desire after Him. We were created for His great pleasure, and therefore, as we live and move and have our being in Christ alone, we bring Him pleasure.

It doesn't matter what label you give yourself or what you tell others about who you are. It doesn't even matter how many platforms you claim or your spectrum of influence. All that matters in the scheme of eternity is whether your heart and life are truly aligned with your Father in heaven, through Jesus Christ. We cannot read one another's hearts, but that is the only thing God looks upon. If you really want to know Him, then you must allow Him to show you how He sees your heart. If we don't recognize our own hypocrisy and repent, Christ is not alive in us—we are merely mimicking Him in our own strength.

The Holy Spirit brings conviction and revelation into our parched souls, and He never lets His own children remain in deception for too long. The goal is not to perfect ourselves or to pull our own weeds from our gardens. We should strive to embrace correction as a gift from the Lord who administers that process within us. This is how we become known by Him and how we learn to love as He loves. The Bible says

God *knows* those who take refuge in Him! Nahum 1:7 (AMP) reads, "The LORD is good, a strength and stronghold in the day of trouble; He knows [He recognizes, cares for, and understands fully] those who take refuge and trust in Him." There will come a day when we will all want to be known by God when we stand before Him.

Sadly, the Scriptures tell us that not everyone who expects to enter into heaven will have the privilege to do so. Matthew 7:21–23 (AMP) makes it pretty clear:

> Not everyone who says to Me, "Lord, Lord," will enter the kingdom of heaven, but only the one who does the will of My Father who is in heaven. Many will say to Me on that day [when I judge them], "Lord, Lord, have we not prophesied in Your name, and driven out demons in Your name, and done many miracles in Your name?" And then I will declare to them publicly, "I never knew you; depart from Me [you are banished from My presence], you who act wickedly [disregarding My commands]."

The definition of knowing God based on Nahum's description is enough to cause any of us to soul search. Jesus said, "This is My commandment: that you love and unselfishly seek the best for one another just as I have loved you" (John 15:12 AMP).

I said it previously, but it's worth repeating: Jesus didn't come to bring peace. He said He came to bring a sword to cut you loose from the things that have invaded your identity and prevented you from loving others due to the deception that once separated you from your Father's heart. He wants to deliver you from all that binds you and keeps you from experiencing your fullest joy, which can only come through Him. Love is not dependence on another human; it is the strength to cover them and represent the love of Christ even when they painfully fail you. Jesus builds His identity in us as He comes in with the winnowing fork to clear away the chaff from the wheat. Our true identity moves closer to Him as it rises to the top (like the wheat), while our counterfeit idolatry (the chaff) is sifted away until our redeemed identity is all that remains, ready to become life bread to a hungry generation.

May we love one another so radically that every demon perpetuating hate, selfishness, and rejection loses its terrifying grip on humanity, enabling wounded healers like you and me to brilliantly pierce the darkness with the colors of heaven. May we be the authentic reflection of the heart of our Father who sent His only Son to light us up in such a way that no one has ever seen! You are loved, and you are called for this amazing time on earth. Together we will reap a harvest that will usher in the return of our Lord and Savior, Jesus Christ, and a time when love will reign over all the damage, all the carnage, and all the pain of the past that we'll remember no more.

Acknowledgments

As I reflect on the abundance of amazing people that God has used to encourage, exhort, and awaken me throughout my life, I am in awe of His strategic design to bring us together in such perfect timing. There is not a day that I am not thankful, first and foremost, for the hand of God at work and for His grace, which is powerful enough to give me something beautiful in exchange for my broken mess.

To my parents who have both made their final journey home, I will always be grateful for the sum of you both that made me who I am, how you taught me about Jesus, and for the gift of music that filled our home, as well as the kind of love that, without a doubt, covered a multitude of sins. The genuine part of our love was tangible, and in the end, it helped my wandering soul to find its home. Thank you for leaving us a legacy of hope that looks for the grace in every situation. I know you both will be at heaven's gate to greet me when it's my turn to cross that threshold. What a day of rejoicing that will be!

To my sister, Cynthia, there is no closer person on this earth who shares my memories, my blood, and my love for singing. We have been given the keys to the kingdom, and together we will take back all that has been stolen from our past. Thank you for releasing me to tell my story. Your sacrifice is a gift of love for others who need hope. I love you, and I need you in my life. "Someone's got to keep it on goin'."

To my daughter, Bryanna Sheree (strong, cherished one), there are no words to express how much I love you. You awakened the better me that was hidden deep within. I thank you for your grace in forgiving me for the hard years and for your willing part in this story. You are a beautiful catalyst, a brilliant butterfly, a truth teller, and my grown-up friend. Greatness lies within you, and I am so proud of the woman you have chosen to become as you too fight forward. What an honor it has been to be your mama!

To my husband, Paul Crouch Jr., the world has yet to see the astounding beauty of your heart like I have! You have a brilliant mind and a true gift for recognizing value in places that most would overlook. Thank you for doing the same with me by looking past my faults in the heaping mounds of yesterday's soil only to recognize the treasure buried beneath the surface. You believe in me and continually inspire me to stretch, grow, and conquer. When I asked God for a prince, I had no idea that He would bring me a king. Together we will continue to heal each other and set "ten thousand" to flight, my love!

To my second dad, Ron Sylvia (Poppie), you will always be a cherished part of our family in the picture of restoration. Thank you for loving our mama like the princess that she truly was and for the selfless love and kindness you have always shown. God is not finished with you. Your best days are still ahead. We love you!

To Dr. Mark Chironna, there was a day when I was withering in a dark little cocoon, and the healing word of your television ministry was the prophetic voice that called me forth from my grave, encouraging me to believe for "what wanted to happen" and teaching me how to fight. I could never have foreseen then that I would someday call you my friend and be enlarged with a vision for the world. Thank you for believing in the Christ in me and for honoring me with your profound foreword for this book. I treasure you dearly!

To Dr. Nick Eno, the day I met you in a coffeehouse to receive your book, *The Orphan Syndrome*, was the day I met a lifelong friend. You have been faithful to encourage and pray for me after the loss of my precious mother when the birthing of a ministry seemed an assignment too great to bear. I would not have made it through this season without your support and friendship. Thank you for seeing the giant slayer in me when I could barely lift my hands.

To Sheila Johnson, the years and miles will never completely separate us. You are forever in my heart and such a significant part of my early journey to healing. Thank you for seeing what I could not see all those years ago and for countless hours of wise counsel over morning coffee and selfless friendship! You will reap the eternal rewards of the seeds you have sown. I love you, forever.

To David Sluka and the entire team at BroadStreet Publishing, thank you for believing in something bigger than me and for your gentle guidance throughout the process of writing this book.

To all the friends and relatives who have loved my family through the years, I thank you in advance for graciously stepping into the light of truth with me where there is no judgment, only mercy and forgiveness. May you forever be impacted by the power of Jesus' blood to transform a broken life and make it beautiful. I love you all.

Endnotes

1   Richard Boyd, "The Impact of Child Sexual Abuse," Energetics Institute, 2010, https://energeticsinstitute.com.au/impact-of-child-sexual-abuse/.

2   Mark Chironna, as provided in an email, dated October 2, 2018.

3   Susan Roth and Elana Newman, "The Process of Coping with Sexual Trauma," *Journal of Traumatic Stress* 4, no. 2 (April 1991): 279–97.

4   Augustine, as cited by Jesse Carey, "15 Augustine Quotes That Helped Shape Modern Christian Thought," *Relevant*, August 28, 2014, https://relevantmagazine.com/god/15-augustine-quotes-helped-shape-modern-christian-thought.

5   Michael E. Kerr, "One Family's Story: A Primer on Bowen Theory," The Bowen Center for the Study of the Family, 2000, https://thebowencenter.org/theory/eight-concepts/.

6   Ibid.

7   Dr. Nick Eno, *The Orphan Syndrome* (Enumclaw, WA: Redemption Press, 2016), 30.

8   *Dictionary.com*, s.v. "tolerate," https://www.dictionary.com/browse/tolerate.

9   Kerr, "One Family's Story."

10 Dr. Caroline Leaf, https://drleaf.com.

11 Dan Rupple, "Projecting Dignity," The Median (blog), April 18, 2018, http://www.mastermediaintl.org/?s=projecting+dignity.

12 Jonathan Cahn, *The Book of Mysteries* (Lake Mary, FL: FrontLine, 2016). The Hebrew Bible actually records the divine name as YHWH, not YHVH. See "Yahweh," in R. Laird Harris, ed., *Theological Wordbook of the Old Testament*, vol. 1 (Chicago: Moody Press, 1980), 210–212.

13 *Dictionary.com*, s.v. "identity," https://www.dictionary.com/browse/identity.

14 John and Paula Sanford, *The Elijah Task* (Lake Mary, FL: Charisma House, 2006), as quoted in Eno, *The Orphan Syndrome*, 107.

15 Oswald Chambers, November 9 entry, "Sacred Service," in James Reimann, ed., *My Utmost for His Highest* (Grand Rapids, MI: Discovery House, 1992) and *My Utmost for His Highest: The Golden Book of Oswald Chambers* (Uhrichsville, OH: Barbour Books, 1993),

16 Harry R. Jackson Jr., *The Truth in Black and White* (Lake Mary, FL: FrontLine, 2008), 94.

About the Author

||||||||||||||||||||||||||||||||||||||||||||||||||||||||||||||||||||

Brenda Crouch is passionate about getting the message of hope and healing out to individuals who are suffering from the physical, emotional, and spiritual prison of abuse or performance-based acceptance. So many are simply trudging through life while marginalizing their true God-given potential because their identities have been hijacked and they don't understand who they are. Her personal search for significance led her to a performance-based identity, which eventually attracted narcissistic, controlling abusers who promised love but never delivered.

Having grown up in the high desert of Nevada, Brenda was exposed to the world of entertainment at an early age. Music was an escape from her feelings of inferiority and shame, stemming from early childhood sexual abuse. Deeply rooted in gospel music, she earned professional status as a singer before the age of twenty. Her stage performances led to the façade of success, and the allure of glimmering lights in the casino industry served to influence her naive dreams. Eventually boasting a career in fashion runway, print, TV spokesmodeling, acting, and voice-over work, her dreams slowly unraveled as God used her pain to expose every dark secret holding her hostage.

It was in her undoing that she discovered a new identity in Christ, which restored her God-given authority after surviving seventeen years of domestic violence and the failure of a second marriage. Alone, broken, and hungry to live beyond empty religion, she devoured the Word of God, which transformed her values and exposed the deception of codependent idolatry in her life.

Brenda's Hebrew name means "sword for the glory of God," and as a weapon forged in fire, she has been prepared for battle against the kingdom of darkness. Brenda's unwavering stance with God's Word makes her a powerful voice anointed to break the sabotaging mindsets of divorce, abandonment, abuse, addiction, inferiority, and pride, giving real answers to both victims and victimizers who want to be free.

As a living example of God's faithfulness, Brenda's powerful testimony confronts the issues plaguing our culture today. Her anointed vulnerability allows the listener to remove their own mask of perfection and face the lies that hold them hostage. She is a TV host, speaker, author, and singer-songwriter who shares this dynamic message of life-changing hope along with her husband, American Christian Broadcaster and film producer Paul Crouch Jr.

Notes

Notes

Notes

Notes

Notes